# TIGHTROPE OF DEPRESSION

# TIGHTROPE

## OF DEPRESSION

*MY JOURNEY FROM DARKNESS, DESPAIR AND DEATH*
*TO LIGHT, LOVE AND LIFE*

## KELLAN FLUCKIGER

New York

# TIGHTROPE OF DEPRESSION
## *MY JOURNEY FROM DARKNESS, DESPAIR AND DEATH TO LIGHT, LOVE AND LIFE*

Published in New York, New York, by Morgan James Publishing. Morgan James and The Entrepreneurial Publisher are trademarks of Morgan James, LLC.
www.MorganJamesPublishing.com

The Morgan James Speakers Group can bring authors to your live event. For more information or to book an event visit The Morgan James Speakers Group at www.TheMorganJamesSpeakersGroup.com.

## Shelfie

A **free** eBook edition is available with the purchase of this print book.

CLEARLY PRINT YOUR NAME ABOVE IN UPPER CASE

**Instructions to claim your free eBook edition:**
1. Download the Shelfie app for Android or iOS
2. Write your name in **UPPER CASE** above
3. Use the Shelfie app to submit a photo
4. Download your eBook to any device

ISBN 978-1-63047-966-4 paperback
ISBN 978-1-63047-967-1 eBook
ISBN 978-1-63047-968-8 hardcover
Library of Congress Control Number:
2016901490

**Cover Design by:**
Chris Treccani
www.3dogdesign.net

**Interior Design by:**
Bonnie Bushman
The Whole Caboodle Graphic Design

In an effort to support local communities, raise awareness and funds, Morgan James Publishing donates a percentage of all book sales for the life of each book to Habitat for Humanity Peninsula and Greater Williamsburg.

Get involved today! Visit
www.MorganJamesBuilds.com

# TABLE OF CONTENTS

# PREFACE

"Recognizing the symptoms of depression is often the biggest hurdle to the diagnosis and treatment of clinical or major depression." Unfortunately, approximately half the people who experience symptoms never do get diagnosed or treated for their illness.

If left untreated, symptoms of clinical or major depression may worsen and last for months or sometimes even years. Not getting treatment can be life threatening.

More than one out of every 10 people battling depression commits suicide. Signs and symptoms of depression include:

- Feelings of helplessness and hopelessness.
- Loss of interest in daily activities.
- Appetite or weight changes.
- Sleep changes.
- Anger or irritability.
- Loss of energy.
- Self-loathing.
- Reckless behavior.

- Having a "death wish," tempting fate by taking risks that could lead to death.
- Thoughts of suicide, suicide attempts.

I'm not an expert at diagnosing or treating depression.

I'm not an expert at understanding all the medical details, causes or current thinking on managing this seemingly increasingly frequent condition. I'm not even sure the frequency is increasing, it just seems like it. Or, maybe it just seems like it because I have it and hate it and am affected by it so much.

I am however an expert at having it and hating it. I'm an expert at running from it, living with it, hiding from it, wondering what to do about it, ignoring it, accommodating it, being debilitated by it and pretending it doesn't exist.

I'm also an expert at having it wreck my life and my relationships, run my every thought and unknowingly direct my goals and actions in an unproductive and often hurtful way.

I don't have a lot of patience with people who tell me how I ought to live. I don't have a lot of patience for people who tell me what I ought to do about it, or what I ought to do because I have it. I have enormous patience and empathy for those who have it or those who live with someone so afflicted.

I have spent my life running from, hiding, medicating and otherwise dealing with this situation.

In my experience, depression is widely and wildly misunderstood. Mostly we ignore it, and once in a while it rears its head in the headlines in the suicide or untimely death of a noted person who succumbs to its siren song.

Then after a few weeks, sympathetic articles, a well-attended funeral and a bit of publicity, it sinks back into the quagmire and oblivion of yesterday's news.

Except, those who have it still have it, and those who live with the infected or afflicted still stand often helplessly by wondering what is wrong with themselves or the loved one so burdened.

This book is not about whining or complaining or wondering why we can't fix this problem yet. I have tried that remedy and it doesn't fix anything, so I quit doing that a long time ago.

## *Why Write a Book?*

If you read this book, you will get several things out of it. You will get an understanding of this condition, from the perspective of one who has battled it for more than 30 years.

You will learn some things that work to help with it and some that don't. Those things may or may not apply to you or those in your life who might be similarly afflicted.

It won't give you all the answers, but it will give you some ideas and some places to start with conversations or processes to manage this condition.

If you have or have had depression, some of the strategies in this book may help you to avoid some pain or some of the symptoms or behaviors that have afflicted me in my course of life.

It may even help you make some changes that give you more hope, freedom, love, power and enjoyment while you continue to figure out how to successfully live with the ebb and flow that always seems to accompany this particular condition.

I don't know what it means to be healed, or how you would even measure such a result. I do know what it feels like to have more or less of this at different times. It comes and goes. Sometimes without warning and with a fierce intensity that is as fearsome as it is unexpected.

The state-of-the-art, at least right now, seems to be a combination of medication and personal ritual that both combats the affliction itself and manages the symptoms.

Sometimes that management is more effective and sometimes less effective but there are ways to mitigate the sometimes confusing and crazy behaviors and feelings of those who find themselves in this condition.

We pretend that we know that depression is an illness.

But we don't pretend it very well. Unless you have been with someone so afflicted, very likely you think someone who's depressed is either lazy, making excuses or just doesn't want to accept responsibility for their own lives. You know, the kind of "suck it up and get with the program" mentality.

That might be a nice way to put people in boxes, but it is wrong and certainly not helpful in managing this particular illness. The easiest way to handle this sort of thing is to ignore it. Unfortunately, this is what results in suicide and broken lives and shattered dreams.

When people have the measles or even a cold, we treat them with all of the best medication and treatment we know, we send them sympathy cards and welcome them back when they're feeling better.

Since we don't really know what causes or cures depression, we pretend like healing it rests squarely on the shoulders of the afflicted and that if they don't get healed in a hurry they must be lazy.

If this description irritates you, I don't care, because it is a prevalent opinion in our current society and somebody has to say that the Emperor has no clothes, so it might as well be me.

I'm writing this book for three reasons:

1.  I need to. I need the catharsis of writing down all of the miserable parts of the journey and the few successful parts that have been with me for decades.

    I have been one of those who blamed myself for everything about this. I was certain that I was not good enough.

    I knew for sure that I was a jerk and that I, and I alone was the only reason that things were unsuccessful in my circumstances.

    I blamed myself for all the relationship problems, breakups and subsequent messes that haunted most of my adult life.

    I need to write this book based on what I have experienced, felt and learned in these decades of painful journey

2.  I'm also writing this book with the hope that it will help two sets of people. Firstly, I hope to help those who have this illness.

    Whether it is moderate or severe, admitted or hidden, diagnosed or merely suspected. Take responsibility for your care.

    Take responsibility to find out why you feel the way you do and why life seems so complicated and hard compared to what you see around you.

    Ignore the nonsense that pours from the lips of uneducated and ignorant fools who offer well-meaning advice and platitudes that sound nice but are nothing more than a reflection of their own ignorance and an indictment of their judgments of your behavior and feelings.

3. The second group I hope to help his those who live with someone who is depressed. That can be a real pain. Depression is not fun, either for one who has it or one who watches.

It is accompanied by ups and downs, unreasonable demands and often annoying, frightening or strange behavior that doesn't make any sense, except in the mind of the afflicted.

Those heroes who have enough patience to love and accommodate those who are ill have always been heroes and continue to be important in creating space and opportunity for those who are ill and those who are on the road to recovery.

Depression, of course, at this time, cannot be healed, only treated with both behavioral and chemical therapies.

It's not hard to understand why it's so complicated, since we don't even know for sure what causes it. Research shows that it may sometimes be related to life events, external circumstances, genetics and perhaps even other things not yet known.

All of these things may cause or contribute to the causes of depression, make it worse or affect it in other ways.

Hopefully you will find the story both entertaining and instructive. I'm going to share the journey that I have made. It's my journey and it reflects my experience and feelings.

I am telling the story without worrying too much about who I offend or whether or not I am able to accurately describe what others are thinking or were thinking at any particular time.

I don't have any space to care about that any more. If I did, the story would remain untold for fear of some reaction which I can no longer conscience.

The best I can do is describe what I saw, experienced and felt. I know for sure that I do not know and cannot understand the motivations, words and behaviors of others any more than they fully understand mine.

With that acknowledgment it is safe to say that this journey is personal and powerful.

I write it now from the perspective of one who is as healed as I know how to be.

Hence the sub-title "My Journey from Darkness, Despair and Death to Light, Love and Life." Those words represent the polar experiences that filled my mind to the point of death and to the point of ecstasy during the complexities of this decade's long journey.

# PROLOGUE

I found myself face down in the carpet. I was behind a locked door in a small study and it was somewhere between two and five in the morning. I was in a lot of pain and couldn't remember exactly how I found myself there, AGAIN.

I was having a conversation with myself. One voice was talking about what an idiot I was, and the responding voice was talking about how I had done a great job ruining my own life.

The interesting part was that 'me', whatever that is, was listening to these two voices talk to each other about what a fool the 'me' in question was.

Wave after wave of anger flowed over me and at the same time a total feeling of helplessness and hopelessness. That combination is particularly lethal. I repeatedly wondered if there was any point in continuing to live.

Then one of the voices would talk about death being a cop out and the other voice would continue to talk about what a great job I had done ruining my life.

The impossible dilemma of the situation seem to repeat itself daily. The only variation were the volume and the tones of voices and the accusations that created the pain. On this night like so many others, I had sought temporary relief through one chemical concoction or another.

You know the old saying, better living through chemistry. And on this night like all of the others, the chemical soothing was only temporary and not really effective.

The dialogue seemed to go on for centuries, although I imagine that it was only a little while. I had no concept of the time passing.

I reflected again and again on how much I was sure that everyone in my life hated me because I was such a worthless piece of crap.

Then the other voice said "you've done a pretty good job of hating yourself, anyway." Then another voice said nobody needs to hate me, I do a plenty good job of that for myself. After a while I lost track of the voices but the cacophony continued unabated until the night passed.

I didn't realize until that moment how many times the same lines could be repeated over and over, hour after hour seemingly with no end in sight.

The fact that external success had come frequently and often to me didn't seem to matter. From an outward point of view I had been very successful and held high positions of authority and power.

My internal struggles were a secret. Guarded because they would reveal the truth that I was a fundamentally flawed person, and above all things, that truth must never emerge into the light of day.

I had never really talked to anyone about the depth and frequency of these episodes of worthlessness, hopelessness and helplessness.

No one would believe me, and since I couldn't fix it, it didn't really matter anyway, right? And anyway at the end of the day who really cares?

All of this time I was actually muttering all of these things out loud, and each of the many voices were sharing a common mouth. After all, the body that housed all these voices still only *had* one mouth. I began to worry that others in the house might hear my multiple pronged monologue.

The world closed in around me, hopelessness became reality and blackness closed in without remorse or relief.

At some point, the realization that it had begun to get light outside entered my consciousness. I knew that the night was over and that I soon had to go to work. Another night had passed without sleep and I knew the day ahead would bring only more misery.

But it was something I had grown used to and I knew that I would get through this day like I had thousands of others before it.

Something was different this time though. I couldn't shake the feeling of anger or worthlessness. I reflected far more deeply on the path of my life and wondered how in the world I had come to this place.

I had been so successful in so many areas, and at the same time so certain that nothing I ever did was good enough.

I found myself in a constant struggle between trying to achieve amazing results, which I did regularly from an external point of view, and at the same time, dealing with knowing that I would never be 'good enough' or receive the approval of those I wanted to please.

Every time success had come, and it had come in great abundance and with great financial rewards, I had managed to destroy both the relationships around me and the situation and opportunities that I had created.

I wanted more than anything else to either die, or to understand what in the world was going on. Why I lived perpetually in such a dark place and constantly felt the need for drugs or alcohol and usually both to self-medicate and hide from the realities around me.

What I knew for sure was that nothing that I was doing was working. Regardless of outward success, my personal reality was at the breaking point.

Everything else was subsumed into one great question. What the hell happened and how did I get here?

Well, it all has to start somewhere, and for me the journey started with the experiences of my warped and wacky childhood.

# PART I

# THE 1ST EPIPHANY, OR HELL IS FOR CHILDREN

I don't really know exactly where depression begins. Based on everything I've read, it's really just educated guess work anyway. I don't know if I have a history of depression in my family - because it has always been one of those secret things that is "illegal" to talk about.

I don't know if there was genetic predisposition or if that question even matters. I don't know if I have some kind of a chemical deficiency or if my depression came from environmental factors or a mixture of all three.

What I do know is that in comparing my memories of childhood now to those that I hear from others, my experience was bizarre. It's not hard for me to see how my childhood experiences might make me answer yes to all of the "Do You Have Depression" questions?

That being said, I now feel quite certain that much of the depression I have suffered for the last decades is a result of environmental factors in childhood experience. That's really a nice way of saying that I was raised in my own corner of hell.

I will never know which experience was the worst or the most causative in the journey. I only know that the sum total of these happenings left me with the fundamental truth: "I Am A Fundamentally Flawed Human Being."

Somehow, the collection of my childhood experiences created decades of depression, cycles of failure and gave me a lifelong struggle with the story of 'not good enough.'

I learned that truth is dangerous and should be avoided, that hiding was required and the living without feeling was the safest place to be.

The journey through of that horror has three parts. Each was a building block to help me create something new. I have called these three parts "The Three Epiphanies."

They were decades apart. With these three revelations, and with the help of God and a wonderful friend who is my wife and companion, I finally have a different place from which to build my view of reality and from which to function in life.

This first section is simply a story about what happened to me from early childhood up to that first grand revelation. I'm going to refrain from blaming or expressing a lot of emotion about it since I'm quite sure nobody intended the outcomes that have come to pass.

So, I'm going to tell it like a story. We will just basically wander through the nightmare of me growing up. I think it's mostly in chronological order.

I've selected a few stories and incidents that I remember either as significant downward turning points, or with such powerful emotional pain that to me at least, it drove me eventually to the place of depression which, as I described above, was "never good enough - or, does anything matter?"

# Chapter 1

# THE END OF THE WORLD

I t was a rainy Saturday, sometime in the late autumn or early winter. I think it was around the first of December.

I was in the car with my parents on the way to my elementary school.

I was in first grade and didn't really know what was going on.

We arrived at the school yard and the place was deserted. I had never been to the school yard on a Saturday and so I had never seen it so quiet and empty. On top of that it was raining and so everything was wet, dark and gray.

I walked down the hall toward the principal's office and my heart was filled with dread. There isn't much in elementary school scarier than having to go to the principal's office. On top of that I was only in the first grade.

I was all alone at the school yard and nothing seemed familiar even though every pillar in the hallway and every building and every bush was in its proper place. Of course my parents didn't count, and I felt completely alone. And, I was on my way to what I assumed were the jaws of death.

Besides the feelings, I don't remember many of the details of that day, but what I do remember is that for the next two hours, and maybe three, I spent time answering questions, playing games and puzzles and doing other unusual activities.

For the entire space of the visit I didn't know what was going on, and didn't understand the purpose of the visit or the questions. After a while, we left and went home without any explanation.

That was on Saturday. The next Monday was the end of the world.

Some people say that the Mayan calendar predicted the end of the world in December of 2012. They missed the date by 50 years. It actually ended on that next Monday in December of 1962.

On that Monday in question I was moved from my first grade class to the advanced track of the second grade. For a few days I thought I was the coolest person in the world.

After all, in my vast experience as a five-year-old, I'd never heard of anyone skipping a grade or a grade and a half, and certainly didn't know anybody that it had happened to.

The excitement faded quickly however. It soon became apparent that I was neither socially nor emotionally equipped to be moved into the older group. I was lost and groping for a sense of stability.

The reality that I was emotionally inadequate was never factored in to the decision and I remained in the advanced placement classes. That continued for the rest of my school experience all the way through high school.

Resentment from other kids was strong and I had no idea how to deal with it. Even after having been moved ahead, I was still reading at least 3 grade levels higher than my class and my other academic skills were also at least one more grade ahead.

But the social and emotional misery far outweighed any momentary excitement I had about having such an advancement.

The rest of that year and in the next couple of years, I tried to make up for my feelings of inadequacy by excelling even more. I became a show-off in both academics and music. As you might well predict, being a show-off never goes over well.

After a couple of years school began to be really miserable and I was completely bored. I began to pay little attention and my grades began to drop precipitously.

I got in trouble at home and punished because of bad grades. I began withdrawing more and more and trying to invent ways to compensate.

## Chapter 2

# LEARNING TO LIE

Because I was usually bored, one of my favorite things to do during school time was to read the encyclopedia. I nearly always had at least one volume of the World Book encyclopedia hidden in my desk, which I read at every opportunity.

It didn't really matter what I was reading about. Sometimes, I would just take a volume and open it to see what wonders were at my fingertips. I read about space, I read about stars, I read about caves.

I read about World War I and World War II. I read about mountains and rivers and oceans. For some reason I always wanted to find the highest mountain, the longest river and the most powerful bombs in existence.

Recess times were always miserable. Not only was I younger than everyone else in my grade but I was also a late bloomer physically. I was smaller and less coordinated than others in the class and consequently chosen last for team sports and pretty awkward at most games.

During recess and lunch time I mainly stood around and waited for class to convene again so I could have something to do that I knew how to do - which was read the encyclopedia.

One of the interesting ways I found to compensate for my social ineptitude was by impressing grown-ups around me with all of the things that I knew. Because I read encyclopedias regularly my head was full of useless trivia that nobody else knew.

I could quote the populations of many large cities and describe in amazing detail the contents of articles about the exact height of mountains, the specific length of rivers and other scientific and natural phenomena.

After a while I realized that nobody knew whether or not the things I said were correct. I began inventing my own facts and stories just for the satisfaction of being looked at as important and knowledgeable.

I realized I could say anything I wanted and no one was the wiser. I began to invent my own facts and figures and created whatever level of recognition I chose with my inventions. This started a long and dangerous affair with compulsive lying.

I withdrew more and more and lived basically in my own little world. That world consisted of books, my own fantasies, and music.

Music, music, music. This played a big role then and plays a big role now. At age 4 or 5 I began to study the piano and began playing musical instruments in the third grade.

Learning musical instruments also came easily. Like almost everything else, I found that I could easily practice less than I was supposed to practice and still perform acceptably.

That led to more compulsive lying. I found it easier and easier to 'get away with' nearly anything. Deeper and deeper it went and as I was 'getting away' with more and more fabrication, it because simple to build my own private world.

This compulsive lying became my best friend and worst enemy.

I got so good at it, that I could convince almost anyone of anything. This is both dangerous and stupid.

Like a Möbius Strip, which is a geometric shape with both sides connected, that ability was both a cause and a result of the oncoming dance of death.

# Chapter 3

# THERE IS ONLY *ONE* WAY

E very parent wants their child to grow up successfully. That definition varies from parent to parent, but mostly it just means parents want their kids to grow up, enjoy a productive life and do things that are good. My parents were no exception.

Usually what happens is parents encourage children to discover their interests, gifts and talents while participating in the structured part of growing up. Ultimately, the child is more or less ready and then they find their own way. Like I said…usually.

My parents, mostly my mom, had other ideas. In her view, there was only ONE way to do literally anything that was the 'right way,' and everything else was wrong. Not different, just wrong.

They married when my mother was very young. She was barely 17. Her mom was a school teacher and gone quite a bit according to my mother's memory of things. The way my mother remembers it, this absence of her mom meant she had considerable 'homemaking experience.'

Basically she had a lot of training in extensive babysitting because she remembers looking after her younger brothers and sisters. However, she was obviously unprepared to guide her own children in a path of finding their own way in the world.

I really don't know a lot about how she was raised. What I do know is that her view of success was to train children to do exactly what she wanted them to do with no exceptions and no deviation.

On top of that, she was devoutly religious and had extreme opinions. These opinions were taught and enforced as dogma and truth, with no room for discussion or deviation.

She was deeply convinced, as most teenagers are, that they know exactly what is right and wrong. She based these views on her interpretation of her faith, and then carried them to an extreme level.

As a kid, you just know that your parents are right about everything. You know that their opinions are true and what they tell you must be the way the world works. So I assumed that my life looked like everyone else's. I assumed that this rigid structure and 'discipline' was the way the world worked.

However my mother's view of things was extreme by any measure and in her worldview, forced compliance to every idea that she had was the appropriate approach to raising kids.

I guess this is a nice way of saying that she was an extraordinary disciplinarian.

By today's standards the 'spankings' that I received would be considered 'beating' and would result in felony child abuse charges and extended jail time. In addition, emotional abuse, verbal abuse and sexual humiliation were also a regular part of the menu.

Perfection was the only standard and nothing short of perfect behavior, perfectly clean rooms and perfectly completed chores around the house were acceptable.

Disobedience was met with screaming, swearing, slapping and of course the dreaded 'spanking spoon.'

All kinds of implements were used for 'spanking' in my growing up years. There were paddles, occasionally a bare hand, pancake flippers, shoes, belts and various other implements. But the most dreaded of all was the 'spanking spoon.'

It may sound quaint and funny now but it was terror incarnate for me as a young boy. It was actually a pierced vegetable serving spoon with a thick, curved, fairly shallow but rigid oval bowl—with holes in it, to let the liquid drain off.

The rigid nature meant of course that it did not bend or flex in any manner and the holes were convenient for leaving welts on my backside, lower back and upper legs.

Mostly, the beatings were aimed at the backside, but given the screaming and squirming the blows often fell off target and landed wherever they landed.

Occasionally, I was spanked through my clothes, but most often I would have to pull down my pants in front of brothers and sisters, and get spanked on bare skin. The bare skin meant of course, even greater welts and wounds.

In addition, face slapping and hitting were common accompaniments with the screaming, swearing and beatings. The favorite name-calling she used was to call me a little 'shit pot.'

# Chapter 4

# THE RELIGION

T hose that know me now, also know that I am devoutly religious.
I was raised in the Mormon tradition and am a 'faithful' member of that church.

For those of you unfamiliar with the Mormon Church, it is a Christian religion that has very distinct and deeply held views about family, why we're here on the earth and the purpose of life.

I still belong to the Mormon Church, but not because I was raised that way. I have been in and out of the church a number of times through the decades and have returned to full activity because the doctrine makes sense to me and I have a deep conviction of its truth.

I have been healed by the Atonement of Jesus Christ.

I don't want to use this book to discuss religion, or the merits of any particular doctrine. I put this section here because some have suggested that there is some sort of causal connection between the Mormon Church, its doctrine and my experience.

I want to be clear, I don't blame the religion or any of its tenants for her behavior. The teachings of the church do NOT support any of the extreme, violent or abusive behavior I experienced.

Her fanatic discipline, her inability to distinguish relative levels of transgression and her unflagging zeal for total perfection and absolute compliance were the foundation for this insane level of discipline.

The issue was not the doctrine of the church, but her extraordinary insistence and enforcement of her own special and unique brand of truth.

# Chapter 5

# REINFORCING THE PROBLEM

So if we go back and reflect on the situation at school, and combine that with the fanatic weirdness of my home life, it's not hard to see why I felt alone, never OK, and mostly afraid.

In retrospect, the big monster for me was a combination of my situation at school as a socially and emotionally immature student way ahead of the class and the wild expectation of perfection at home.

I remember looking forward to going every day to school. I loved learning, and I loved to be gone from the house so I would not get in trouble.

While I was at school, I was isolated but safe and I felt like school was a little place where I could escape fear and pain by hiding in the books and encyclopedias I read.

I also learned to create some grudging acceptance by impressing those around me with memorized facts, reading skill and fanciful lies.

This witch's brew slowly and subtly reinforced the truth that came to govern me in every piece of my life—both at school, and at home—that I was sub-human and beyond redemption.

From a social point of view, I was a social outcast at school and at church, the butt of jokes with my horn-rimmed glasses, and hiking boots, shunned and chosen last, etc. You know the type.

I internalized the truth that I was inadequate, not good enough and that nothing I ever did would be sufficient to gain either the friendship of people at school or the approval of my mother.

Every day, this slid me deeper and deeper into depressive sadness and a desperate desire to have somebody 'like me.'

I remember fearing the slap and the spoon from my mom so greatly that I lied all the time about everything. I was so terrified that lying became the preferred alternative because it let me control my life in a small measure.

Of course the consequence for lying meant that I often got in double trouble. It seemed that whatever happened I got punished twice. I heard 'tell the truth— it's better to face the truth than lie...' a million times, but it never seemed to make any sense.

I knew that the 'double trouble' would happen, but sometimes it didn't and I got away with stuff. Even sometimes outrageous things. On top of that, I was so scared that any punishment I could put off to the future would be better than getting it today, no matter how bad the future beating might be.

So, the reality was that most of the time my transgressions, offenses *and* the lies were discovered. That meant I got to double-dip; I got spanked for whatever I did wrong and on top of that spanked because I had lied.

At school, you could at least ask questions. At home, my mom was so convinced of her moral correctness and superiority that she enforced every preference that she had with the same zeal as a religious principle.

I have often reflected since then that as a child I never understood the difference between 'preference' and 'principle.'

For example, I grew up thinking that jazz was evil and of the devil just because she said so. With every aspect of life, she was opinionated and unyielding. This meant in my world certain attitudes and opinions were sinful just because she said so.

I was well into adulthood before I even began to consider that this outrageous approach to childrearing and teaching was not only wrong, but harmful and damaging. There will be much more on that later.

I clearly remember today several periods in my life where I was getting spanked every day. I remember sitting in my room wondering if I could get to the next day without a spanking. It often left me wondering: Why was I so incapable of pleasing anyone in my life?

# Chapter 6

# MY DAD

U p to now, I have spoken exclusively about my mom. My dad was there, but the contrast between the two of them was stark and confusing.

He was the one who seemed to 'be there' even though he was less physically present. His presence was usually more fun and I enjoyed trying to do the things that he did, like any boy who wants to grow up to be their dad.

My dad often 'worked late.' I didn't really understand what was going on, but about 3 pm nearly every day, the phone would ring and my mom would tell us that 'daddy is working late.'

I accepted this without question, and simply did see him until the next morning for a few minutes before he was off to work. I often felt like my dad was treated badly by my mom.

Her attitude was impatient and condescending sometimes I felt anger towards her, but mostly it was just life, and life was just like it was.

As it turns out, there were other things going on at the time between them that I still do not know about, even to this day.

While my father participated to some degree in the violence and abuse and his punishment was also harsh, it was nothing compared with the wrath of my mom.

Once in a while, she pulled the 'I will tell your dad when he gets home' thing and I remember once or twice getting whipped with a belt late at night.

Even though it only happened a few times, I remember lying awake in bed after it was dark and dreading the moment he would come home. Again, I don't remember why I was in trouble, I just remember waiting.

After a while, I heard him come in, and then a quiet conversation ensued. After a bit, my dad came and got me and took be to get whipped with a belt. I was really sad.

While I do have recollections of extreme and cruel punishment from my dad, it was far, far rarer and my feeling about him was much different than for my mom. Much less fear, much more connection.

She was the big violent monster in my mind.

# Chapter 7

# THE FIGHT

W hile I remember less violence and fear surrounding my dad, I did sense tension between them. It was behind the scenes, but it was there. Sometimes the 'working late' was a trigger, and sometimes just other tensions in the air.

My mom and dad did not fight that much where we could see them. Their arguments were kept private for the most part. There was one dramatic physical fight and I will never forget that day.

It was terrifying. I heard the shouting and then I saw them chasing each other around the house. It was violent and extreme. They ran into the garage and then I couldn't see any more although I could still hear the shouting.

Later, I saw the outcome. There were marks on both of them, and I remember what I thought was a black eye on one or both. I remember knowing that it was awful, but thinking that it was the same as I got…

The fight was violent and serious, and I know they were worried about what I had seen. There was a long and awkward silence around the house after the fight for a few hours.

Later, they each came separately to ask me what I had seen. I stuttered and stammered and told them what they wanted to hear. I don't remember what I said, but I know I was scared.

# Chapter 8

# THE REBELLION

I t's funny how that all works. Even though I knew punishment would come, I began to look for ways that I could be disobedient and get away with it.

Because everything was structured and rigid, I never felt that I had any freedom of my own to act according to anything that I wanted to do, so I looked for ways to 'get away with' disobedience.

Somehow, even though I was terrified out of my mind of the beatings, I was also feeling the seeds of rebellion. I gloried in the chance to 'do something wrong' and not get hit.

This combination produced sneaky and lying behavior at home and more and more poor performance at school. My grades began to drop and I stopped doing homework at all.

I think it was the fourth grade that I even got a C- in one subject. In our system of measurement at home, that amounted to a triple F. And that does not mean "fortissimo" except for the accompanying punishment.

This resulted in a very complicated and strange dance. I lied every time I opened my mouth. I would never admit to anything because of the fear of punishment, yet I continued to cheat everywhere I could.

I lived in terrible guilt all the time with all the things I had lied about or 'gotten away with' flying as a bright red flag of 'sin' and burning in my mind. I think my mom knew that something was wrong, but could not deal with it in a normal way.

So she invented a new twist.

Chapter 9

# THE "BAD SESSION"

S he started something I named the 'bad session.' Perhaps sensing that there were things not right having no way to unravel the mystery, about once a year we would do something akin to 'confession.'

Out of the blue, my mom would ask me if there were 'sins' I had not 'confessed' to her. She did it without yelling and in a different sort of mood.

This was something like the function of a confessor priest. When she started this new system and would ask these questions I was horrified beyond words. I expected that if I confessed anything I would be excessively beaten.

As it turned out, in these particular and exceptional cases, which happened without warning and without predictability, things were different.

I never understood what caused this strange day to come around. But on these days, something shifted in my mother and she would listen to whatever I said without reaction.

The result of this odd dynamic was that I would lie always about everything that I did to avoid as many spankings as possible. And then hope that those weird "confession days," would allow me to empty all the lies I had stored for so long.

My plan to eliminate spanking didn't work, but it did allow me to escape some punishment and beating that I'm sure I otherwise would have endured.

This bizarre ritual taught me a lot about lying and hiding and nothing about honesty, truth, Christianity, or living any kind of faith in any consistent way.

The combination of this extraordinary physical punishment and my experience as an outcast at school left me totally isolated with no one to talk to. I was alone, afraid, and certain that life was weird.

The only confidant I had my entire life growing up was my younger brother, four years my junior. We used to make each other promise that we would 'never tell' anyone about certain escapades.

Kind of like brothers would normally do. For a while, we actually kept our promises to keep things secret. But my mother's overwhelming personality would override such promises. My younger brother would be made to feel wrong for keeping confidences and would confess for me.

Then I would be 'spanked' even worse. Once for the actual deeds, once for lying and then most of all for extracting such a promise from my younger brother and teaching him such evil behavior.

# Chapter 10

# SWEARING

M y grades at school suffered because of the collective trauma. My behavior at school suffered as well. I stopped doing homework and regularly lied at home and at school. I claimed at home that I didn't have any homework, and at school, I just kept saying it would come later.

I didn't turn in projects and big assignments and the teacher had no idea what to make of the situation. She knew I was smart, could easily do the work and got good grades on tests. But homework was out of the question.

I was feeling isolated and afraid and at the same time wanting to lash out in the most desperate ways. I regularly did silly and crazy things like peeing on the floor in the school bathroom. I intentionally broke things I thought I could get away with.

I took up swearing. I would swear at school as often and as fiercely as I could. It got so bad that the other kids didn't want to be around me because my mouth was so foul.

I viewed it as a sign of power because it was the only kind of rebellion I thought I might get away with because I thought there was certainly no way my parents could find out.

I could not have been more wrong. One day I got home from school and I had an angry mom waiting for me wanting to know why she had gotten a phone call from school about my filthy language.

I then of course got grilled about how I talked. She demanded a complete report about exactly and precisely each word that I had said. I lied about that, but I had to give enough examples to satisfy a reason for the frantic call from the school.

Then after the grilling and the total explosion about my language, she wanted to know why in the world my mouth was so filthy they needed to call home. Especially when I 'knew much better' than that.

Of course that resulted in a tumultuous number of lies and eventual spankings and other forms of exotic punishment.

It did not cure the swearing in any way shape or form. I just became more careful about who heard me. It became one of my primary forms of rebellion because it was one of the few things I seemed to be able to get away with, if I was careful.

# Chapter 11

# DISTRACTIONS

I buried myself in reading at school. Often reading books that had nothing to do with what was going on in class, I often got in trouble because I had a book at my desk to read while the teacher was talking. I daydreamed incessantly and continued reading encyclopedias and other reference books.

As many young boys do I became infatuated with "the Hardy boys" mystery series. For me it was a welcome relief into a fantasy world that seemed so exotic and safe. I counted every one of them that I had read.

I memorized the number of volumes in the series and kept track of the numbers printed on the volumes. At one point, I could mostly recite the names, numbers and plots of all of the books I had read.

I tried desperately to get more books in the series. I exhausted the supply in my elementary school library. In frequent trips to the large public library in our community there was a bonanza and I was able to gather more books.

I expanded beyond that series and took up reading of anything and everything as a welcome relief from the weird life I somehow thought was normal.

I kept looking for other ways to demonstrate rebellion. Again, my natural talents provided the answer. I mentioned music a few chapters ago, and it too, played a role in both distraction and rebellion.

Because I love music and had some natural talent, I took up several instruments. In 3rd grade I played the tuba. In 4th grade I started the French horn. In 5th grade I added the clarinet. In 6th grade I added the trumpet.

This was in addition to the piano, which I had been playing since I was four years old. All those instruments was the fun part and the distraction.

The rebellion came afterwards. I began lying about practicing. Not because I didn't like to practice, but because I could get away with lying and still do well in the band and at school.

I find it interesting that music has become an essential and enormous part of my life. I have played professionally for many years and have operated a recording studio on and off for the better part of 35 years.

It is often caused me serious reflection since then that something so powerful and important to me was also the source of rebellion and avoidance behavior simply so that I could have something that I could control.

# Chapter 12

# HOMEWORK

L ying and getting away with not practicing my musical instruments was fairly easy. Lying about homework and assignments was another story entirely.

There were many large projects at school that I simply never started and, if I had had my way, never would have completed. Two stories will suffice to illustrate the point.

The first was a report on Switzerland assigned in the fifth grade. Everyone in the class was assigned to write a report on a particular country. It was a typical elementary school report.

It was supposed to cover the people, the geography, the history, the languages, the economy and all of the usual things that would be discussed in a fifth grade school report. It was a big deal and assigned for several weeks of the quarter.

I picked Switzerland because my last name, Fluckiger, is Swiss and it made sense to me. I had never been there but had fantasized about it. I loved the pictures of snow-covered Alps and beautiful green mountainsides and the legacy of a strong and independent people.

I never even started the report. I read everything in the school encyclopedias about the land. I did make some halfhearted attempts at school to make some notes, but that was all. I never even informed my parents that we had an assignment, what I had chosen or that such a report was due.

It was a big deal because it was large and would make up a significant part of our grade. I just didn't care. I wasn't going to do it.

Of course that plot failed miserably. Funny how little you understand as a kid. Kind of like pretending that someone can't see you when your head is under the covers.

After I lied repeatedly to the teacher about it 'being home' and 'almost being done,' the inevitable happened. One day my mother pulled up at school. I saw the car coming and nearly died. Of course, she had been called by the teacher. A conference ensued and of course I was in deep doo-doo.

I spent the entire weekend preparing the report. We had been given several weeks to prepare it, but I was able to do it quickly. It was a good report and the teacher said it would have earned a good grade. But of course being weeks late the great I got was marked down significantly.

That of course didn't help my standing at home either.

# Chapter 13

# THE NAZIS

T he final example is a little odd. It did involve failing to complete homework or anything else. It was a time where I learned the power of symbols and learned that there were others besides my mom who had strong views.

I didn't really understand what was going on at first. At some point in my voracious reading, I became infatuated with the stories of World War II. I loved to read about the equipment, the airplanes, the tanks and all the other machinery of war.

I read everything I could find, and memorized the names of battles and generals, who had the biggest guns and who were the most feared leaders. Of course, I had no real context to understand war and its terror except my own private battlefields.

In particular, I found myself attracted to Nazi Germany. I don't know why. It may have been that the regimented and fanatical system felt similar to the life that I lived and somehow it spoke to me as a familiar feeling.

In process of time, I also became infatuated with the swastika symbol. I drew it all over my notebooks and textbooks at school. That did not go over well.

This behavior produced a violent reaction in the teacher of that class. She got after me and repeatedly told me to quit drawing the symbol. Of course, I had no real knowledge of what the symbol meant or the emotion such a powerful symbol would evoke.

I don't know what the personal experience of that teacher was. She may have had memories of loved ones involved in that horrific period of history. In any case, I ignored her instructions and continued to draw the symbol bigger and bolder on everything I could find.

Again, I was in deep trouble. Another phone call to my mom resulted in another mid-day visit to the school and the associated terror. I also was assigned big report I had to write about the swastika, what it stood for and what had happened in WWII.

While I learned a lot more about what really happened in World War II, my fear came from the consequences on the home front. I learned that those in power can do anything they want, and when you are weak, you suck it up and suffer.

# Chapter 14

# SPAGHETTI

My feeling about my dad is confusing and contradictory. I don't remember him being as violent as my mom. At least nowhere near as often.

In a previous chapter, I said that his discipline was harsh but infrequent. There is one incident that I remember clearly where he lost all control. It is stark, brutal and clear in my memory.

This all happened in front of the whole family.

I don't remember exactly how old I was. I think I was about 11 or 12 years old based on other memories that I have before and after the incident.

We were sitting at dinner as a family in the kitchen around the table. I was seated at his left hand on the side of the table next to the wall.

I don't remember what happened to start the rage. There was no shouting ahead of time, so I think it was something I said. His reaction was sudden and frightening.

He smashed his left hand in the back of my head and my face landed in the plate of spaghetti in front of me.

He then yanked me up from the table and dragged me around to the other side of the table. He stood up and kicked me in the backside as hard as he could.

He then proceeded to kick me out of the kitchen, down the hall and all the way to my bedroom.

He probably kicked me seven or eight times on the trip down the hall. Once we got to my room he continued to kick me all the way across my room and into the corner by the closet.

I run out of room and was against the wall.

He continued to kick me and I felt like a Jack-in-the-Box going up and down against the wall as he kicked me from behind.

I was screaming. He was shouting at me the entire time but of course I can't remember anything that was said.

The terror of that day was burned in my mind forever.

I couldn't understand why I was such a rotten person that I deserved such fierce punishment.

# Chapter 15

# THE TRACTOR

M y experimentation with drugs as a means of escape from reality and a relief from the tone of my life started really early in my life. It was by accident, but it started a long chemical romance.

An interesting part of my growing up was that each summer in my younger years as soon as school was out we would make a trip to my grandfather's farm in Wyoming.

This was something dearly treasured since it gave me many, many hours away from my mother's tyranny and a number of other adults to interact with on a close basis. My favorite of course was my uncle who ran the farm and was buying it from my grandfather.

He used to tell us all kinds of stories about his growing up and things that he felt strongly about. He was patriotic and told stories about heroism and bravery. He taught us cow punching songs and stories about cowboys and farm life.

I eagerly spent time in the barn every morning and night at milking time. I loved the chores and the feeling there and the whole experience. It was literally a godsend as a break from the normal routine.

My mom was busy helping with other work around the farm and chores in the house. That meant that we were much less supervised and my younger brother and I wildly enjoyed for those few weeks in the summer. It felt like a tiny piece of childhood that might be considered normal.

While we were there we fed pigs and calves, we rode horses and milked cows. We mended fences and we hauled hay. I'm sure we were a lot less help than we thought we were, but for a short few weeks we felt like we did something useful.

Though the farm work was sometimes rigorous it was outdoors and a lot of fun. The spankings were a lot less. Even at the time, I had the sense that my mom spanked us less because she was embarrassed to do it so much in front of others.

Boy was I grateful for the 'others.'

It was on this farm that I had my first introduction to drugs and it was quite by accident.

All the farms in the area had their own gas and diesel tanks to keep the farm machinery running. One day while filling the tractor with gasoline at the large tank that stood out by the barn, the smell of gas going into the tractor tank was quite strong.

I had always found gasoline to have a pleasant odor as opposed to some people who find it offensive, so I just stood by during the filling process without thinking much about it.

I did not breathe it in on purpose but I did not move away as the tank was filling. By the time the tank was full I was quite lightheaded, and I experienced the first feeling of what it was like to "get high."

For a while I didn't really understand what had happened. The temporary intoxication wore off and I forgot about it for a few hours. Later that day I reflected on what had happened and guessed that the gas fumes might have been the cause.

That also started an entirely new set of experiences in my life. All summer long I snuck opportunities to open the gas cap on the tractor and "sniff gasoline." Once or twice my uncle knew something was wrong, but he could not pinpoint the problem.

By then I was in the seventh grade and that would've been about 1967. We lived in the San Francisco Bay area. Being the center of the hippie movement, the talk of drugs was everywhere.

I began sniffing gasoline from the gas can in my parent's garage on a regular basis. My dad kept a can of gas around for the lawnmower. We normally used the push mower on the grass and occasionally we were allowed to use the power mower. So the gas was always there.

Sniffing gasoline and getting high became one means of escape from the brutality that continued at home.

You would think that by the time a boy was 12 years old that his mom and dad would have ended beatings as the primary form of discipline.

This is not the case with me. Like I described earlier, I was physically a late bloomer. This meant that I was fairly small and very late reaching puberty. In middle school, spankings were still a common form of discipline. That continued all the way into high school.

So I added sniffing gas to the list of rebellions I committed at every turn. These rebellious activities consisted mostly of stealing candy from stores, sniffing gasoline and disobeying at every possible opportunity.

I knew the consequences if I got caught, but the pressure to act out was intense. Fear was rampant in my life and again during this period of time I remember thinking often that I got spanked every day.

I was ashamed of the amount that I got spanked so of course, I never told anyone what was going on at my house. I was sure I was a complete failure as a person and totally not good enough to measure up to anyone's expectation so it was my fault anyway.

# Chapter 16

# MY DAD AND CIGARETTES

n about the seventh grade, I was let in on the family's 'dirty little secret.' One day my mom took me aside and in the most furtive and secretive of ways told me that my dad was a smoker.

I was also instructed that under no circumstances was I ever to discuss this with anyone for any reason. I was simply being told so I knew the 'truth.' I was surprised because all of this had been completely hidden from the kids.

The health dangers of smoking were not yet in the public eye, and it was still a glamorous attraction in movies, magazines and television for kids growing up to sneak cigarettes. I had not yet had my first puff, but many of my friends had tried cigarettes and some were furtive smokers.

My dad had picked up a habit of smoking in the Army years earlier when he served during the Korean War. I was also told that my older sister had been told a few years earlier and now it was my turn to be part of the inner circle.

For my mother this dreaded habit was a real cross to bear.

The habit is so dreaded because in the Mormon Church smoking is forbidden and prevents one from going to the temple.

For her, the represented possible eternal death and damnation. Not for her, but for my dad.

In the Mormon tradition, this habit was very serious and often people were ostracized or treated badly for these breaches. I can only imagine the embarrassment, stress and pressure this must have created for my mom.

Given her rigid views, this must have been mind blowing. I am sure she felt isolated and alone in bearing that burden and in trying to keep it from public knowledge.

In retrospect, being freaked out about my dad may have been one of many stresses on her that caused her to be so cruel to me as a growing child. She was going to make sure that I didn't do any of that awful stuff. If only it were so easy as that.

It's funny, when she told me about his smoking, she told me she was letting me in on the secret because eventually I would smell it on his breath. When she said that, I vaguely remembered asking my dad or my mom some days earlier why his breath smelled funny. Maybe that was the trigger.

I don't remember feeling worried about my dad. It just introduced another layer of uncertainty and weirdness around the house. You know, sort of like, 'wow, dad does stuff…' What does that mean for me? I really only remember being more scared.

I never knew if my dad got told which of the kids knew and which ones didn't. We weren't allowed to talk to each other about it at all. It was just another secret that was hidden even though anything we did seemed like it was never hidden. Weird.

Not too much later in one of my gas sniffing episodes, my dad thought I was acting strangely. I probably was, since when he asked me if something was wrong, I was in fact, high on gasoline.

He demanded that I come close so he could smell my breath. I was terrified out of my mind and absolutely certain that the world was going to end.

In retrospect, of course he was trying to see if I had been drinking booze. That vice had not yet entered the picture of my life, so there was no smell of alcohol to detect.

I guess the odor of gasoline was not strong enough to set off any alarm bells. And I am equally sure that the thought of me sniffing gas to get high and escape never crossed his mind.

Par for the course. I never knew when I was going to get caught and spanked or when I was going to get away with anything. The result of course, was constant turmoil and fear.

A year or so later, my dad actually finally kicked the habit and quit smoking. We knew something was happening because he was acting differently, and after a year clean, he was allowed to go to the temple. My mom and dad exchanged new rings and rededicated themselves to each other. I remember thinking that was cool.

## Chapter 17

# MAYBE I COULD DIE

So by now I know you are sick of hearing about the discipline and humiliation. Me too. You might wonder why there are so many stories devoted to the different situations. It was a big part of my life.

I devote so much time and describe so many examples of the physical abuse because it shaped me in amazing ways and constituted so much of my life at that time. In fact, between the actual spanking and the fear of the spankings it makes up many of the significant memories of my childhood.

My largest memory of childhood is fear of my mom, and many of the situations I remember were centered on choices I made which were 'wrong' in her book and for which I then got slapped, screamed at or beat as a consequence.

Another strong memory is something that I frequently thought about and wished for during the punishment sessions and afterwards during the screaming and crying.

In one of the periods when I was sure I was getting spanked every day for weeks on end, I remember wishing during each spanking that I would die. You know, the old 'wish for death to end the torture scenario.'

The sad thing was that I was not wishing to die as a relief from the torture, but I was wishing for death because I thought that if I died my parents would get in trouble for my death.

In the weird brain of a child it never occurred to me that I could ask for help.

So I never told anyone about the beatings and simply wished over and over again that I would die in the process so that they would get punished for their actions.

Another frequent thought during those years was that I should be gone from that house. I thought often about running away. I even experimentally ran away a few times when my mom was gone from the house.

I didn't have a plan and I had one to turn to. The real problem was I was too scared of the beating I would get when I was caught and would have to come back.

Again, the notion of simply asking for help never crossed my mind. Strange how that works. I remember one particular night when I decided I would really run away. My dad was working late and my mom was gone somewhere.

I was the oldest one home with just my younger brother. In the end, I could not leave him alone, so I came home and waited for death to come again.

The most horrific memory I have about spanking centered on one of these times. My mom and dad were gone to different places and my older sister was also somewhere else.

My younger brother and I were home alone and we went outside at night to play with the neighborhood kids for a while. I talked about leaving again, but in the end, chickened out.

We then came back inside and knew that we were going to catch hell when my mom got home. I told my younger brother again I was going to run away because I didn't want the beating that I knew would come.

He promised he wouldn't tell so I stayed. Something I had done clued my mother in that I had been outside. So the first thing that happened when she got home was that she dragged us both in the kitchen and asked us if we had been outside.

Despite the fact that I was an accomplished liar at this point, the terror in my brother's face gave everything away. I will remember that night as long as I live.

My brother was spanked moderately. And then sent to bed so that he would not witness what would follow. My mom then proceeded to beat the shit out of me. She beat me into a corner in the kitchen and then continue to flail away with that spanking spoon until I was a screaming heap on the floor.

I determined then the running away might actually be a viable option. I was so terrified I couldn't think. But the next morning came, and things were back to 'normal' and the reality of nowhere to go set in.

I had no friends to whom I could turn. We had no relatives in nearby towns and so the prospects for successfully running away were effectively nil in my small and terrified view of the world.

# Chapter 18

# ONE SMALL CHANGE

n the middle of the seventh grade I decided that I no longer wanted bad grades. The year did not start well, but something happened that made me change my mind.

I got in trouble again, and I was sitting in the school counselor's office waiting for something to happen. I was alone, and the counselor had stepped out to check on something. My school file folder was laying on the desk.

You know, that 'secret' file they keep on you that you never got to see as a kid. I picked up mine and started reading it. The results of all the IQ tests we had taken over the years were listed and I saw my numbers.

I was shocked at what I saw, and decided that I should do something besides get bad grades. There were several scores from different years, but all of them were between 162 and 164. I wasn't sure what that meant, but it seemed high. I decided that from then on I would get straight A's.

In addition, my older sister had been getting good grades in high school and I know that I could outperform her. This might be a way to get the approval I craved after all.

Besides, failing to do assignments and getting in trouble perpetually wasn't working and it was time to try something else.

In addition to the punishment I got for bad grades, I somehow began to sense that bad grades were going to hurt me later. So starting with the seventh grade all that changed.

Being able to do the work was never an issue. It just occurred to me that refusing to do my homework was going to hurt me more than any satisfaction I got from the rebellion.

So even though the grades went up, there were other things that I got into trouble for. I think around that time, the neighborhood boys created a stash of playboy magazines. Pretty typical stuff.

But you can imagine in my world that girlie pictures were not part of the menu, they were the flaming gateway to hell. I remember once being told by my parents that they would cut my penis off if I didn't stop reading such filth. Same game, different pieces.

# Chapter 19

# KEEPING A JOURNAL

A round this time I was required to start keeping a journal. It wasn't an idea that I had, but I am glad that it was something I was forced to do. I guess there's some small truth to the nonsense of 'you'll thank me later.' At least in this very limited sense.

I remember never writing in my journal what I actually felt. I knew without a doubt that my parents, particularly my mom, would take my journal and read it anyway.

I didn't even have to ask. There was no such thing as privacy in our home. I remember asking my mom if my journal was private, and the look I got was incredulous beyond measure. I never asked again.

I knew that some of the other kids at church and at school kept journals and I would ask them if theirs was private they assured me that they had privacy and that their parents would never violate that trust.

I wondered why that was such a difference between my family situation and theirs. I even was bold enough to ask on one occasion. My mom's response was typical.

She told me that the other parents were all wrong and that they shouldn't allow that privacy to those children because they would certainly do evil with the right to privacy in a journal.

This is another example of that idiotic but pervasive 'preference' versus 'principle' framework where her fear translated some imaginary principle of religion into a fanatic rule that needed to be enforced with violence if necessary.

The reason I remember the journal with fondness is not because I ever wrote anything true in there, but because the act of writing a journal gave me time to think about what I actually felt.

Even though I could not write anything real in the journal, I was able to think about what I was feeling and experiencing for the first time and start to wonder what the heck was wrong with the universe I lived in.

Even though I was terrified to actually ever write anything in the journal that even resembled the truth of what I felt about anything, I remember the feeling of longing to keep a record of my days and life.

I considered trying to create a code, I considered trying to have a secret journal. In the end, I knew it was futile and so I just played the game.

It was during these times of deep reflection that I really felt the deep tug of what I would later come to recognize as depression. The sadness was overwhelming. The hopelessness and the helplessness.

There were three reasons I didn't want my journal read. First of all, it was mine and I wanted it private. Second, I did not trust my feelings. I was sure that I was 'bad' and I did not want that 'weakness' and 'imperfection' disclosed.

I had many questions. I was sometimes angry, and sometimes fearful, doubtful and confused and I did not want her to know that because it meant I was weak and evil.

The third was a more practical reason. I assumed also that if I wrote anything about my treatment at home that violent consequences would be the outcome. On top of that, it would also include loss of whatever privileges I might have.

So the journal became a quiet time for reflection. This turned out to be useful even though actually writing anything real in a journal was absolutely out of the question.

Because I knew she was reading what I wrote, It also became a game for me to write crap that I thought would impress her with 'just enough' rebellious tint to sound like a teenager, but mild enough to avoid violent consequence. I was also able to express a degree of the sadness, fear and loneliness that I felt as an outcast at both school and at church.

None of that ever had any perceivable effect on the course of my life, but it was cathartic to make the attempt. I could daydream and live in a place of exploration and no fear.

The actual sad and true consequence of all of this was not good. I lived in a shell world. I went through daily motions doing what I needed to do to be safe, stuff my fear and anger and lie enough to impress people and keep mostly out of trouble except when I didn't.

I kept getting good grades because it was safe. I had no meaningful relationships at school, church or at home. I was firmly convinced that nothing I ever did would be good enough. I knew for sure that I had failure written all over my life and that everything about me was doomed to miserable banishment.

Chapter 20

# THE LOCKER ROOM

---

When I got in high school I was both excited and scared. High School was cool, right? But mostly I was really scared. I was nowhere near puberty, small and insecure.

I was completely withdrawn from any social contact with nearly anyone. As I noted, my relationships at school, church and in the neighborhood were shallow and few.

My parents enforced that isolation even in the church by curtailing participation in activities and reminding me continually that all the other parents were wicked because they allowed their children to do things that were contrary to "right and truth."

The leaders were wrong, the parents were out of order and they was the sole defenders of the true faith. And, because of her righteousness, I would be protected from evil.

I say my 'parents,' but I should be more specific. While my dad was peripherally involved, it was really my mother and her warped insistence on being 'right' in every respect.

Specifically, I was forbidden to participate in any youth activities that went anywhere overnight, because that was evil and I would surely do bad things. So again, I missed out a lot.

Of course, the overnight activities were the ones that were the most fun, had the most excitement and the most social opportunity.

Because I was such an outcast at school, the other high school boys picked on me. That would come as no surprise to anyone that knows the nature of high school. I got shoved around a lot and picked on in the locker room.

One incident in particular will illustrate the point. There was a fellow who lived around the corner from me named Dennis. He had bright red hair like I did.

Because he had red hair I felt something in common with him although I didn't really have much of a relationship with any of the kids in the neighborhood. We were kept away from them because of their "evil natures."

One day in the locker room, I think it was 10$^{th}$ grade, Dennis walked towards me and suddenly punched me right in the face. No warning, no quarrel, no issue whatsoever. I was shocked and obviously it hurt badly. The boys looking on laughed.

I learned later that they had made a bet the Dennis wouldn't do that. Of course, as any high school boy would do to win the bet, he walked up and punched me right in the face. Given my nature to hide everything I was too frightened to go complain. Besides, I thought it would make me look weak.

It's simply further added to my certainty that I was worthless and not good enough in every respect. I mean after all, who in the world walk up and punch someone in the face if they were worth anything, right? Of course, I didn't tell anyone and made up lies about the bruise.

Thankfully, there is only one final incident of physical abuse that I will describe. This one really is a powerful memory and is the other one that I will never forget. I remember this because not only was it painful but it caused so much embarrassment.

After one particularly bad beating at home, I remember hiding in the locker room and waiting until all of the other boys were changed into gym clothes and out on the field.

I then looked furtively around to make sure no one was there and changed quickly. That meant that I was late out on the field which of course got me more reprimands but I didn't care.

The reason I was late intentionally was that I was black and blue on the backside, lower back and upper legs, as usual. This had resulted from a particularly severe application from the good old "spanking spoon."

I don't remember what the 'sin' was, but whatever it was, it had left red welts and black and blue marks all over my backside. And of course I didn't want anyone to see that because I was embarrassed at having been so worthless as to receive such a beating.

## Chapter 21

# THE BROKEN PADDLE

Oddly enough, there was finally an end to the physical abuse. When I was in the 11th grade, again I had done something outside the lines. I don't remember what it was, but it merited severe punishment like most misbehavior did.

I was required to wait in the laundry room of the house while my father went out and actually made a paddle out of wood. I had to wait with my pants down because I was going to receive a beating on my bare butt.

It took several minutes to create the paddle. After the paddle was formed my dad came in to use it and proceeded to swat me as hard as he could. I simply ignored it.

After a few swats the paddle broke and I stood up and looked with a defiant stare into his face. I remember his words very clearly. "Well, I didn't expect you to cry, but…"

Obviously, that was the end of the physical punishment since it had become useless. Interesting to note that I can't remember what any of the infractions were, but the incidents of beating are clearly burned into my mind in all their gory detail.

At the end of the day, the end of the physical punishment did not mark a change in any attitudes. It simply was a recognition that it was ineffective and pointless at this juncture.

I had also begun to feel physically strong enough that I was prepared to get in a fight with either of them and I believe they began to sense that.

So although the physical abuse stopped, the overarching certainty that I was an inadequate person in every respect, was clearly still the order of the day.

It is not surprising that it left a permanent mark on me that I had to deal with for decades.

Again, the deep pull of sadness, uselessness and inadequacy that I would later come to know as depression was a constant nagging pain tugging at my heart. I stared out the window often, trapped and wishing to die.

# Chapter 22

# BE STILL AND KNOW THAT I AM GOD

Amidst all this turmoil, there was one very bright light. I was raised in a religious home but the religion was twisted and brutally applied.

Not surprisingly, this made me wonder if there was such a thing as a real God anyway. One day, in total desperation, I determined to find out.

After one brutal exchange with my mom, which left me smarting a little from the slap to the face but hurting deeply because she had once again attacked my worth by calling me names; I stood at the window and stared at the sky.

I cried out loud 'Are you there? ' Do you even exist? Is there such a thing as a God? What am I doing wrong to get physically and emotionally abused and punished every single day of my life?

'If you're there I need to know.'

For the first time in my life, a sweet peace flooded over me and words formed in my mind. These were words I found later in the Scriptures in a couple of places. They said simply "Be still, and know that I am God."

The terror passed.

Life did not change for me. It was just as awful and my mom was just as big a monster. But from that day on I knew there was a God, without a doubt. And that someday something would change.

# Chapter 23

# THE PIANO OR "IT'S ONLY HIGH SCHOOL"

P hysical punishment stopped in the 11th grade. Insane, but true. The upshot was great fear and a sense of worthlessness, coupled with a sense of defiance.

The effects spilled over into everything I did. I was always afraid my papers, tests and performances of any kind would be sub-par and subject to ridicule and/or punishment

This led to a massive effort to over-achieve so that somebody somewhere would tell me I was OK. Internal validation was not an option, and the desperate search for external approval was in full bloom. That went on for decades.

There are a few incidents that were powerful in shaping me because they reinforced my need for external validation coupled with the underlying certainty of inadequacy.

Maybe you feel the same way?

Music was a godsend. It began to play a larger and larger part of my life principally, as a place of refuge from the confusion and depression of my growing up experience.

It would've been glorious if I had received some affirmation that what I was doing was good, but even without that it was a powerful positive force for me.

I have been playing the piano since I was four years old and had become quite good at it. In my senior year of high school I was asked to play a duet with solo piano and orchestra. The piece that was selected was George Gershwin's Rhapsody in Blue.

Those of you that know the music know that it is very difficult. I practiced hours and hours. I was excited and was able to play it well. It was a great show-off piece and I loved it.

However, when the time came to perform my fear of being 'not good enough' trumped my preparation. I played most of it well, but there was one part where I made some obvious mistakes.

It didn't wreck the performance but it certainly was not what I had wished for. I was quite depressed. I received no affirmations from my family. You would expect that your loved ones would pump you up, clap you on the back, and tell you it was good and make things ok, right? Never in my world.

The mistakes were real and the embarrassment was real. I know for certain that my fear of failure caused the panic and mistakes in the clutch.

On top of that, the director said to me afterwards "well, it's only high school." I'm sure he meant well and if I had been healthy in my head I would've heard it that way. As it was, it felt like further affirmation that I sucked, would always suck and that nothing could be done about it.

## Chapter 24

# BEING SMART IS ALSO BAD

A nother interesting incident involved music as well. I played the trumpet in the jazz band. We played a number of pieces that year that featured screaming trumpets playing way up high.

Playing the screaming trumpet part was the fantasy of every trumpet player and we had a couple of guys that could do it. The stratosphere on the trumpet was not my forte.

We always used to sit around and listen to the original band that had recorded the music so that we could lust after their outrageous performance.

One day while sitting around listening to the Maynard Ferguson band wail on the high notes, I enthusiastically commented on the screaming trumpet parts by saying "wow, listen to that double high C."

Everything went quiet and the others looked at me and asked, 'How do you know that was a double-high C?' I froze and wanted to crawl under a chair. I meekly replied, 'I don't know, it just sounds like one.' Immediately, someone ran to the piano to find out if it was correct, and it was.

What I didn't know was that no one else in the room could hear a note and know immediately what was. I didn't realize that others could not do that. I was blessed with a high degree of talent with respect to my ear and perfect pitch and so forth.

That incident caused me enormous embarrassment, and I felt really guilty because I thought I had done something wrong.

Again, just the flavor of my entire outlook on life. I never said anything again about notes. I felt that somehow I would be singled out and have less chance of being accepted because I was odd.

I was also writing my own music by that time, but I played it for many people because I was afraid that it would be rejected. That would demonstrate again that I was a failure.

Not much of a beginning for a performing artist.

# Chapter 25

# THE PICTURE

omewhere in the final years of high school I remember one other incident that shaped my march to depression in a powerful way. It involved a simple family picture.

The picture was black-and-white and was just a normal picture of my older sister, myself and my younger brother.

This group of three kids represented the 'first kid group' in our family. The 'second kid group' came along 7 years later and also had three kids in it.

My older sister, my younger brother and I were separated by about four years each, so it's not difficult to imagine what the picture looked like. Three normal little kids in a black and white picture appropriate for about 1962 or 1963.

My hair was combed up in a wave that stood up above my forehead, which was how I wore my hair until I was 11 or 12.

The trauma came from a conversation about the picture. I don't remember what started the conversation, but given what was said I'm certain that I had been disobedient about something, and therefore was unacceptable.

On that day, my mom said something to me that hurt me and stuck with me forever. She looked at the picture and said that somehow there had been a dramatic change in me shortly after that picture was taken.

She told me, referring to that picture, where I must've been about six or seven, that at that time I was innocent and obedient and a "good boy."

She said 'I don't understand what happened, but after that time you became selfish, disobedient and no longer the innocent little boy in the picture.' Well, she was right. She had seen to that.

Kids grow up and change, that's the normal course of life. But that comment struck me to the core and simply reinforced the fact that in her view I had become, and always would be: disobedient, selfish, dishonest, unacceptable, not good enough, rotten, unworthy and every other disgusting and repulsive adjective.

Like everything else, it simply went into the bank of truth and I accepted it as the framework for defining my life at that time.

One more step down the ladder of despair and into the pit of depression.

# Chapter 26

# THE EVIL GIRL FRIEND

My parents' unflagging effort to control effort to control and dominate every aspect of my life knew practically no bounds. In the last part of my senior year in high school I dated a girl named Jo Ellen.

We had two dates. She had expressed some positive feelings toward me and given me a small gift. We agreed to 'think about' each other at 9:30pm each night to have a mental connection. This was way out of control for my mom.

Even though she was of our faith, my parents were worried that we would somehow become seriously involved and forbade me to see her for two months. They called a meeting.

They asked me to bring her to the house. We had a formal meeting in my parents' bedroom. They were very serious. They made me promise them, in front of her, that I would not see her, or communicate in any way, for two months. She had to promise the same thing. For our own good.

Obviously, the answer was rebellion. I snuck away at work and rode my bike to a pay phone and called her anyway. But they won, in that it ruined the relationship.

What did I learn? I can't be trusted, it is OK to embarrass and humiliate a kid in front of a friend, friends are used to manipulate you and I am inherently evil.

One more chorus of 'not good enough.'

## Chapter 27

# OFF TO COLLEGE

graduated from high school with an extremely high grade point average and received a scholarship to a college located 1000 miles away. I was wildly relieved to be getting out of the house. This brought to a close this traumatic and terrible episode of my life.

The stage was set to move to the next phase. The firm learning I had was simply this: that under all circumstances and no matter what happened, I was not to be trusted and under no circumstances could I be good enough.

Maybe you know that song...

I had no idea what a college experience might look like. I supposed that I could make my way forward but I also knew with equal certainty that somehow I was fundamentally flawed.

I accepted as a given that regardless of any accomplishment I would never measure up and receive the approval of those whose approval I craved most desperately.

I guess it's one of those weird syndromes where you seek the approval and desperately need the affirmation from those who never under any circumstances, will provide that for you.

What I remember most of all is that finally I would be able to act without fear of immediate consequence. I relished the thought of simply being able to walk around campus without somebody asking about every thought, word or breath.

The first thing I did was go buy a couple of records that I knew would have made my mom furious because they were evil. Wow, such rebellion.

It's also interesting that this method of raising me was a 'perfect storm.' A set-up for decades of depression came from her crazy desire to 'protect' me from evil.

In her mind, she set about preparing me for the world by having absolute control over everything I did growing up. That way I would be protected.

Obviously, the exact opposite would turn out to be true.

# Chapter 28

# THE EMPTY HALL

I arrived at my freshman year of college a couple of days early. I was staying in the dormitory on campus that year, and because I was early, the dormitory was empty. I happened to be on the top floor in the hallway that had about 30 rooms on both sides.

It seemed like a long hallway to me. After I had put my belongings in the shared room I had been assigned, I stood outside the door and gazed toward the other end.

Not a soul in sight and not a sound greeted my ears. It seemed unnaturally quiet, and my recollection is I never heard it that quiet again the entire year. I remember standing there for a long time for some reason and thinking about what lay ahead.

The depression must have been particularly strong at that moment because I thought gloomily "I'm younger than everybody here, I'm still 17 and I won't be 18 for several months. This is really going to suck."

I stood there swimming in my misery for several minutes and then a thought came to me.

It came like a flash of enlightenment. It literally felt like a bolt of lightning had struck me on the head from out of the blue. I ascribed it then and still do as some sort of divine intervention in my life.

The thought was very simple, but it changed everything. 'These people who are coming to fill these rooms have never seen me. They don't know anything about me.

They do not know that I am an introverted, bookworm, awkward, socially inept nerd who can't get a date, doesn't know anything about social graces and has never had any friends.

What if I don't tell them?'

What if I don't tell them? The words resonated like thunder through my mind. I realized that they would have no basis for forming any judgments except what I told them and what they saw on their own.

What if, at that very second, I changed everything and began acting in a completely different way?

What if I acted self-assured, like I had been popular, like I knew what I was doing and like I was likable, important, and worth knowing?

The thought terrified and excited me at the same time. I had no idea how I would create such an impression, but I certainly knew without a single sliver of doubt that if I could, the old Kellan would disappear forever and the new one would exist, simply because I decided it to be so.

I made a vow at that moment to create that reality starting that instant. It felt like I was actually creating a fantastic and elaborate lie, or was it?

As you might expect, it was not easy to suddenly change all of the behaviors I had become accustomed to. So I'm sure my 'performance' was far from perfect. But the outcome of my sudden epiphany and determination to act completely differently worked in the most extraordinary fashion.

From that second on I 'became' someone else. I was able to get to know people, people were appreciative of my gifts and talents, I was able to make friends—with girls no less, and get dates and be a normal freshman in college.

"I AM IN CONTROL."

By itself, the statement may seem a bit clumsy. And doesn't even begin to capture the nuances of the truth. It is obviously not true in an absolute sense. But in a rudimentary way, I realized that I could create the world around me.

Coming from the place of feeling no control at all over anything I thought, did or said it was a staggering revelation. You might think that an epiphany of this magnitude would somehow completely right the ship of my life that was listing badly and taking on water.

What was missing was me having an understanding of the depth of the dysfunctionality created by my warped upbringing. There is no doubt whatsoever that I was not equipped to be in possession of such power.

My self-concept was still on founded on the bedrock of depression and the certainty that I was fundamentally flawed and worthless. I was simply going to hide that fact from everyone.

No one will ever again know I am worthless.

## PART II

# THE 2^{ND} EPIPHANY OR LIFE IS WORTH LIVING

Even with all the shortcomings, that simple thought that "I AM IN CONTOL" helped me to create an entirely new universe. I was excited and dizzy at the same time.

To start with, it was more a rebellion from all of the things that I did not want and things I wished had not happened to me before. Unfortunately, the newfound realization that I was in control did nothing to get rid of the feeling that I was not good enough.

I now had freedom to do everything wrong. I took advantage of that freedom. This new control let me create a future more like I thought I wanted, but what I wanted had no boundaries, common sense or future picture of success.

A mix of "I am in control" with "I am fundamentally flawed," is an obvious train wreck waiting to happen. And it did.

I was on academic scholarship. That meant I needed good grades. I got straight A's primarily because getting A's in class required little effort, even in the honors program. I'm not sure if that intellectual blessing is a curse or a gift but it was simply the truth.

I dated excessively, stayed out all night, spent an enormous amount of money buying "forbidden music" and basically set about raising all the hell that I could.

Toward the end of my freshman year I began heavy experimentation with drugs again which I had let go for the first two thirds of the school year.

I got in all kinds of trouble, but it was trouble of my own making and so that was somehow different. Since I was by definition "fundamentally flawed," what difference did it make what havoc I created?

My personal life was a shambles for the whole year.

I guess that's not much different from the first 17 years of my life, but at least this was shambles of my own making. The nagging feeling of worthlessness was still there, waiting in the shadows and temporarily silenced by the noise of the party,

The terrifying truth for me now was that I could create anything I wanted, I could cover it with lies and my natural ability and in this fashion I could hide my total worthlessness under the blanket of distraction and achievement.

After all, I stood there in the hallway and realized that I could create my own future. That meant that everything after this should be easy, right?

Anyone living in the real world knows this is not true.

You might want to ask yourself at this point if any of these realizations or truths resonate with the conditions of your life. My lack of understanding how things actually were led to great suffering and a lot of pain for me and those around me for the next 35 years.

In hindsight, the pivot point of many problems lay in the contradiction of the two fundamentals I held to be true. The juxtaposition of "I Am In Control" and I Am Fundamentally Flawed" led me through a gigantic roller coaster of horror.

One manifestation of this paradox was that each time something was not easy or completely successful, I immediately reverted to the knowledge that 'I was not good enough.'

The next logical step meant that being 'In Control' simply meant I had the ability to create fabulous illusion.

For the next three and one-half decades, undiagnosed and untreated depression drove me over and over again to bounce between major success, sometimes on the world stage, and falling just as precipitously to splatter on the concrete below.

The staggering cost of this crazy dance with self-loathing dragged on through multiple marriages, business ventures, damaged relationships with family and friends and stints in hospitals and rehab centers.

The stories are different and sometimes almost unbelievable, but after a while they all start to feel the same. The weirdness is the same, only the faces change.

Come with me and lets move roughly chronologically through these decades and I will share some of the highlights and lowlights of the journey, picking incidents that illustrated different facets of the trauma, drama and madness.

I know many of these stories will feel like pages from your own diary, and I hope the insights are helpful in your own private war.

# Chapter 29

# MARTIAL ARTS

K ung-Fu, with actor David Carradine was a popular program growing up and at least where we lived there was huge interest in the martial arts. I had no opportunity growing up to pursue that interest, but now that I was 'In Control,' I began to look for ways to learn.

I could not afford formal training at that time so I bought all of the books and videos that I could and spent as much time practicing I could possibly manage. I became extremely limber and worked out hard. I felt very dedicated and worked at it for seemingly endless hours.

I suppose there are many reasons I was so attracted to the martial arts. I felt it gave me control and power. I felt like it made me 'cool.' It made me feel some degree of personal affirmation which was so lacking in my life.

In any case, the physical demands and work felt good, like it was something I could be good at. I was a late bloomer as I mentioned, but with this rigorous work which included stretching, self-taught martial arts and distance running, I started to feel good.

At the end of that first year, I ran a 20 mile race. That was the longest race I ever ran. I'm not sure why I never ran a marathon which is only a few more miles but I didn't.

I don't think I have the physical equipment to be a champion distance runner but I forced myself to run many miles for many months so that I would develop the kind of stamina I imagined I needed for excellence in martial arts.

At the same time, I played volleyball for the University volleyball team, second string, and in that capacity got to meet the former US men's Olympic coach and a former US Olympic player who were the coaches for the University team.

After working on these things for nearly a year, as fortune would have it I met a martial arts instructor in the area. I explained to him what I had been doing on my own and ask him if he would do me a favor.

I asked if he would watch me do some martial arts moves and then judge my level of competence. I wanted to know how 'good' I was from someone outside myself. I asked if he could tell me what belt level I might have achieved in his school.

I guess the old script of 'not good enough' was still the prominent feature of my internal architecture. So I needed somebody to tell me I was okay.

His reaction was interesting but not really surprising. 'People can't teach themselves martial arts. Most people have no idea how to do it, don't ever get limber enough and can't do anything very well even though they might think they are cool,' was his reply.

That was depressing but I persisted and ask if he would look at it anyway and be honest and tell me what it looked like so that I would have some idea what I had done. To my surprise, he agreed.

I demonstrated the techniques I knew. I had only learned some of the formal exercise and content that accompany formal martial arts training, so I knew it was only partial at best. I did the best I could.

He watched carefully and considered what I had done. He then told me that he was surprised at what I had learned and that my demonstrated level of proficiency was about that of a brown belt in his school.

I was ecstatic. A brown belt is one level below black, which of course is the ultimate macho ideal of everyone who ever thinks about the martial arts. Even though it did not mean I had earned that rank, or that I was entitled to wear a brown belt, it was an awesome boost to my feeling of control.

This reinforced the epiphany I had had at the beginning of the year and reinforced strongly the powerful knowledge that I was in control.

Unfortunately, I didn't understand what I really was in control of. And the revelation did not come with the wisdom nor the tools to deal with the fundamental feeling that I was 'not good enough' and never would be.

## Chapter 30

# MEDITATION

At the same time as my love affair with martial arts started, I also became deeply engrossed with the idea of meditation and inner exploration.

I voraciously read everything I could get my hands on regarding meditation, self-hypnosis, and other mind control methods that presumably gave access to further control and greater power.

I practiced mind-control techniques, visualization, memory enhancement methods and various disciplines of meditation. I also started dabbling in the occult and paranormal techniques. That was scary. I saw and experienced things that I never want to see again.

Whether or not you believe in the occult or spiritual things, I know from my own experience that there are both good and terrifying powers that are beyond our normal senses and that are eagerly trying to influence our behavior and lives.

I didn't really understand the drive to do this at the time, but in retrospect, it seems like I was just looking for ways to be something besides a pawn in somebody else's game. Who was I, what did I mean, and can I really be something of myself?

Combining meditation and martial arts was a theme that stayed with me for decades. I used meditation techniques to enhance learning abilities and reading speeds.

I found that these mind exercises were effective for learning faster and better retention. This meant that grades at school got even easier.

Meditation and mind control techniques served me well throughout my life. They still play a big role in leading a sane and complete life with my depression under control.

Much later in life I wrote a series of five books teaching the beginner how to meditate and use this wonderful tool to create space and sanity amidst the noise.

I also use meditation as a powerful tool to help clients now with their drive to create results and to find discipline and order in the chaos that sometimes surrounds us.

## Chapter 31

# THE MAGIC OF THE MUSIC

---

I f there was magic in my life, it was in the music. From my earliest recollection, I loved it. Partly because it gave a something to be 'good' at and show off with, and partly just because it was what it was.

All the way along the thorny path of growing up, music was fun. I cheated on my practicing because I could, but it never dampened my love of the expression.

Continuing in college, it provided release and joy. In the second semester of my freshman year and all the way through my sophomore year I was in a performing/touring group called 'Sounds Of Freedom.'

We performed a mixture of patriotic, family and popular music consistent with both high quality and family oriented fun and entertainment. The show was a 90 minute variety show consisting of singing, dancing and some skit comedy.

I was in the orchestra that accompanied the group. It was a small orchestra consisting of a rhythm section a piano and some brass wind instruments. I was one of the two trumpet players.

We performed on campus, around the community and had a 10 day tour during the semester. We also recorded an album. The tour was a lot of fun, because I got to miss a week of classes and associate with a good group of people who enjoyed music as much as I did.

Everywhere we played, the audience would always ask for autographs which made me feel like a minor celebrity. At the same time because of how frightened and unworthy I had felt most of my life it gave me a strange and challenging experience.

Because the program was sponsored by the University, all of the professors knew about the traveling groups and made accommodations for our absence from class by giving us a homework to take with us and allowing us to makeup exams.

Some professors were nicer about it than others, but overall it was set up well and it worked well. I don't really think any of this affected any of my grades.

This opportunity solidified one truth deep in my heart. Music was really one of my most powerful callings and creative outlets.

This turns out to be really important. Today, music is pivotal for me still. Two albums are accompanying the writing of this book. Music reaches our hearts like nothing else.

In a few chapters I will describe a fateful decision that dramatically increased the depth and power of my depression. It involves an abandonment of this knowledge that I am full of music and must create it. But that is yet to come.

Back to the touring group. Occasionally, at certain venues, the band for the group would not break down at the end of the performance. Instead we would hang around and play some current popular music for the audience. Effectively, it was an impromptu dance for audience members who hung around. For me, that was fun. Really fun.

It was all contemporary pop music and if essentially it was a bunch of musicians jamming after the gig. During those jam sessions, I didn't play trumpet. Instead, I played the piano.

The pianist for the group couldn't play by ear and I knew many of the pop tunes of the day so I switched from trumpet to piano for the dance tunes.

I think this meant so much to me because it was almost like being a mini-rock star. It felt like the first time in my life I got attention in a positive way. Imagine this: I had just signed a bunch of autographs and the teenagers and young adults in the audience hung around to dance while we played pop tunes.

Of course, that made us even more popular. It was a wildly new and strange experience in my universe.

The highlight of the two years was a 30 day tour that we took after my sophomore year. We went all through Colorado, Utah, New Mexico, Georgia, Louisiana, Florida, Texas, Oklahoma and probably a couple of other states.

We played a concert nearly every night so that meant nearly 30 performances on the tour. It was my first longish road trip. It was exhilarating and I never wanted it to end.

The most fun we had was at a performance was in Lubbock, Texas—of all places. It rained so hard during the performance that all the roads were closed and none of the audiences could leave for an hour or so after the show.

Of course that meant we had to play another dance. Everybody had fun, the water went down and the audience finally went home.

During my freshman and sophomore years at school I also took several music classes. Music theory and some composition. I did well in the classes.

The skill that I had with my ear that I talked about earlier came in very handy and so again, I was something of a standout in the class.

So here is the dichotomy, these two years really awakened a desire to pursue a musical career. Because of the negative feelings of my mom about music, I didn't do it.

I know it seems insane that some kid in college is too scared to study the things he wants to but that's how it was. Fear, even away from her ruled the context of my life.

Instead, I majored in mathematics for a while, and then tried out accounting. I got straight A's in both, but I knew I would die if I turned into an accountant. I also learned a little extra money as a math tutor since I was a year ahead in calculus, because I took college classes while attending high school.

Being in the touring group, my skill at the piano plus my newfound power from the epiphany gave me the ability to create some "bragging rights" for myself.

At the same time, not being skilled in any of the social graces, I was actually an awkward clod socially. Instead of creating charisma, it was just a kid who was trying to show off.

That didn't help me win friends and influence people.

# Chapter 32

# THE NEW EVIL GIRLFRIEND

istory repeats itself, often in the most bizarre ways.

Partway through my freshman year, because I had learned that I was "In Control,' I started dating. I was able to get dates here and there, but my mental backdrop was weird.

I lived in the land of unworthy so profoundly that any date was great, and any attention was good attention, right?

This is not unusual for socially awkward boys, and I felt like the poster child.

The problem was that my bedrock unworthiness left me yearning for any approval and attention. This meant I would go with any girl and 'fall in love' just to be wanted.

I got a girlfriend and we dated steadily and heavily. I lied about this to my parents and then they somehow found out. That did not go over over well.

The relationship with my parents became strained. They were angry that I had started dating and picked up a girlfriend. They were certain I was going to hell. And a visit home at Christmas time was extremely stressful and short.

Because I was in the touring group and was still using a very old trumpet I got in junior high, my girlfriend wanted to get me a new horn. My mom desperately wanted that NOT to happen. That girl would then own me because I would owe her.

I remember the trip well. We went to Salt Lake City, and visited several stores. We got a beautiful horn that I used for 15 years. It was a memorable trip and a great experience, except for the thorn…

With strain at an all-time high, I didn't visit home again for a year and a half. After that Christmas break, my freshman year, I went back to school, threw myself into studies, continued to get straight A's, do music, play an 'evil' trumpet, have an 'evil' girlfriend and make more messes.

At the end of the freshman year, I started experimenting with drugs again, fairly heavily. This was directly attributable to the strain at home.

I didn't have summer yet organized, and I was afraid to go home, so I sought refuge in drugs. Again. Finally, a summer job became available at the farm of a relative in Star Valley.

I jumped on that in an instant. Summer passed and I was back at the University.

## Chapter 33

# THE SECOND YEAR AND WHERE ARE WE?

The second year at school was different from the first in one important way. I was trying to start deciding for myself what I wanted to do and not do.

Locked in the inevitable struggle between self-determination and the iron-fist of self-doubt and 'not good enough,' I just barely stayed afloat.

I was stuck between knowing that "I am in control," and not having a clue how to use that knowledge in a sensible and socially acceptable way.

I quit using drugs. I got good grades. I was in a touring group doing something I loved, but at every turn, I was rejected and discouraged from the home front.

I craved affirmation from my mom. In my framework, she was the bedrock source of truth and righteousness. Without her blessing, I was still nothing.

I was angry, rebellious and still stuck on the truth that somehow I must win her approval to be 'OK.' This made for a volatile and unstable combination.

The bottom line was this: my first two years of college were simply an escape from the tyranny of my upbringing, but afforded me no real solid ground to create a path forward.

I was living under that repeating refrain "you're not good enough and never will be."

# Chapter 34

# TO SERVE OR NOT TO SERVE

---

S o, I find myself at the end of two years of college. I had a scholarship waiting for me for the next year, I had just completed a 30 day musical tour with a performing group.

I felt so beaten-down I did not dare tell my parents I wanted to pursue music as a career. Initial conversations on this subject met big resistance. My mom was certain that any such career would lead to a life of immorality and destruction.

After all, all rock and pop stars had long hair, played evil music, were evil and used drugs, right?

My college experience taught me one thing besides "I am in control," it taught me that I never wanted to be at home again.

As it turned out, that was never going to be an issue.

In the Mormon Church, 19-year-old boys serve a two-year mission to proselyte for the faith. I was not yet liberated enough from the tyranny of my upbringing to decide anything for myself. I felt compelled to serve the mission, even though I hated the lack of control I felt.

At the same time, I felt something positive in my heart about the doctrine and precepts of the Mormon Church. As I mentioned earlier, I am still devoted and active, even though I have had several periods of my life completely away from the church.

The thought of serving in a foreign country or somewhere interesting was appealing. I also looked at the opportunity to go on a mission as a chance to be gone away and on my own for two more years.

It is interesting now, to see the conflict of that time through different eyes. I had the beginnings of my own conviction, and rebelled at the same time from the force my mom exerted.

In the end, the parental control, the nascent conviction and the desire to be away won out, and I decided to go on a mission.

I spent two months at home after the 30-day musical prior to entering my mission August 9th 1975.

Chapter 35

# MAN ON A MISSION

The two months at home between the end of my musical tour and leaving on a mission were full of activity and the busyness of preparation for leaving. I had a full-time job working for a contract painter and so even though I stayed at the house, I thankfully wasn't home much.

I was called to Northern Belgium for my two-year missionary service. Northern Belgium speaks Flemish, which is a variation of Dutch. The written languages are the same but if you ask a 'Vlaming'—(a resident of Flanders—Northern Belgium) if he speaks Dutch, he will tell you "NO."

I attended two months of intensive language training in Rexburg, Idaho at Ricks College. Learning a new language was fun and intense and something I was pretty good at. Wow, something I did well!

For me, it felt a lot like hearing musical intervals and I was able to learn quickly and easily. It wasn't very long after I got to Belgium that I began to be known for my excellent Flemish.

Getting rid of the American accent was easy because it was just like music. You make the sound coming out of your mouth and in your ears match the sound of a native.

For some reason it was natural and easy for me and I realized I had somewhat of an affinity for languages. This created another crazy fight in my head.

I began to be renowned, even within 6 months for my command of the language, and particularly the pronunciation. It was rumored that I had the accent of a native. I struggled with that, both basking in the 'glory' and feeling unworthy of the attention.

I learned the language well and quickly memorized all of the materials we were given to prepare us for proselyting work.

Missionary work in the part of the country that we served in was all Flemish. The southern half of Belgium speaks French and Belgium is essentially a bilingual nation so it was not uncommon for us to run into French-speaking people.

Because I felt proficient in Flemish, I wanted to learn French, because I thought I could be more effective. I also suspected that sometimes people responded in French because they could, and actually didn't want to be bothered with a couple of missionaries trying to tell them about a new religion.

The mission rules were very specific and very strict. This kept us focused and safe. Learning another language was against the rules and we were directed to use all our time in the work at hand.

I found that rule to be silly and so I followed my own path. Perhaps because I was still creating rebellion just so that I could get away with something. That was only the first of many things that led me down a path of rebellion and breaking the rules.

For the most part I was a hard-working missionary and performed the service well. But the unresolved monstrosity in my life of 'never having control' led me to break rules and do things according to my own plan, which was contrary to the mission expectations.

I started writing to girls in the mission and forming 'pen-pal' relationships. However distant these may seem as you write letters, it is pretty stupid to create any relationship like that. As a missionary from America you are certainly not seen in a "normal" light by the people interact with.

Even though I was 'mostly diligent,' I know that my lack of stability and the internal conflict created by breaking rules I had committed to affected me deeply.

I know that much of the mission that I served was hampered by the vacillations between breaking rules and performing in an extraordinary fashion. I certainly did not make the most out of my time during that two years.

The pattern of extraordinary achievement followed by self-sabotage and self-loathing was to form a pattern and a refrain that repeated over the next 35 years.

It has since caused me deep reflection that I was prevented from using the obvious gifts and talents that I had to their full advantage, because I was so crippled by the belief that I was not allowed to be a success.

Nothing about the missionary activity or the religious doctrine caused me any issues. In fact today, I am a devout member of the church. But the totally rotten foundation upon which my emotional buildings were built caused me to bounce outside the boundaries all the time.

I mention this again because I get asked all the time if I think that the church rules, doctrine or practices caused my problems. No, I don't feel that way.

There was one incredible bright spot during this time. Because of my training and talent, musical opportunities abounded. I was regularly able to serve using the musical skills that I had.

On my mission I had my first concert performance. I composed and performed an original piece in front of about 2000 people. It was exciting, fun and made me more certain than ever that I wanted to compose and perform music as my life's passion.

I also met a young couple during my mission who ran an antique shop. They did it because they loved what they did and it made them happy. This also made a powerful impression on me.

It added to the growing certainty that music was what I wanted to pursue and that nothing should stop me from that dream.

Of course, this was in direct opposition to the powerful messaging I had received in my upbringing and caused me enormous emotional conflict.

The battle was just beginning.

# Chapter 36

# FALLING OFF MY FIRST CLIFF

I mentioned creating relationships with girls that were in the mission where I served. This is strictly forbidden by the mission rules for several reasons.

First of all, as missionaries you look different than 'normal' people. You have a special purpose and status. This has an attraction and makes it easy for local girls to be attracted to you.

My own personal insecurity and need for affirmation trumped following the rules. I took advantage of the attraction and allowed myself to flirt and ultimately be attracted to girls both in the 'pen pal' way and in person in areas where I was stationed.

I was asking for trouble and I got it. Near the end of the two years I served, I created a relationship with a girl in a city I served in. I knew her superficially from church, but not much else.

I started sneaking out at night to visit her, and of course, eventually I got caught. Finally, my lack of following the rules reached catastrophic proportions.

I got excommunicated from the church and sent home. It is ironic that I actually served a few days more than the two years I had been called to serve. But I came home disgraced nonetheless.

It was the most painful thing that I had ever experienced. I was terrified at the thought of meeting them because I knew that they would be angry, hurt, disappointed and sad. I knew my mom was outraged.

For me, all the years of independence melted away in seconds. I was again a little kid, totally in terror of my mom, believing that she had power of life and death over not only my physical self, by my spiritual being as well.

In the longest plane ride of my life, two years and two weeks after I had left, I flew home to San Francisco and was picked up by my family at the airport.

Not much was said at the airport, but the feelings were palpable. I was a total failure, an embarrassment, and everything that had ever been thought, said or indicated about my being "not good enough" had absolutely come true in a wildly devastating self-fulfilling prophecy.

We create our reality from what we believe. I believed I was worthless. I believed that no matter what I did, I was 'not good enough.' I believed to the core of my soul every accomplishment was a tiny grain of sand stacked against a mountain of wickedness and evil.

I shriveled into the darkness and despair of self-loathing and depression.

# Chapter 37

# REJECTION, OR $260 AND A BUS TICKET

T he consequences and future direction of my life became quickly evident. The very few days I spent at home were uncomfortable and negative. My parents, particularly my mom, made it very clear that I was not welcome there.

It wasn't very long before they told me that I needed to leave. Even though I had a waiting scholarship, I could not go back to the school that I had been attending, because I was excommunicated from the church.

In order to attend Brigham Young University you have to have a letter of recommendation from the bishop in your home ward. Having been cut off and expelled from the church for my conduct, I could no longer get such a recommendation.

I had no idea what I would do or where I would go. In the most awesome and fearsome rejection I have ever experienced I was basically given a one-way bus ticket to Sacramento. This was about 90 minutes from where we lived.

I was also 'given' the $260 which was the total amount remaining in my bank account.

I had a one-way bus ticket, $260 and one suitcase with some meager belongings. End of story. Of course I never returned home.

Unfortunately, the anger and rejection I felt was smaller than the guilt and conviction that I was evil, worthless and had been sent away to vanish or die.

The ensuing decades brought about bad decisions, and huge oscillations between world-stage highs and rehab lows. I was not equipped to understand what to do next or where to turn.

Unfortunately, the big drive was to prove something, not to me, but to my mom. I desperately wanted to prove she was wrong, be 'good' and 'get back into the fold.' This was the bane of the next 35 years.

It trashed my life and injured others all around me with the shrapnel. The sad story will be revealed as the next several chapters unfold.

I took that bus ride with no idea where I would go, who I would see or what the future for my life would be like. I was alone. Utterly and completely alone.

I went to the only place I knew, which was the LDS employment services. They were gracious enough to give me some recommendations of places to look and I ended up getting a job as a laborer at a 7-Up bottling plant.

I worked at that plant successfully for a few months and quickly was promoted to machine operator and made a little bit more money. Even though I was emotionally a wreck, my natural gifts and talents made it easy for me to get promoted.

While working for the 7up factory, I made the acquaintance of a fellow whose dad was a manager at the local electric utility. Pacific Gas & Electric Company.

On the recommendation of his son, my co-worker, I went to visit him for an interview. That fateful and seemingly random act shaped the next 30 years of my life. In truth, there are no accidents, but it seemed very random at the time.

I had never had the slightest interest in utilities, electricity or anything to do with that. Funny how a random interview, or perhaps a divinely directed opportunity, shaped and directed my life for the next three decades.

Depression has a funny way of ripping your heart out and smashing your face in when you don't expect it. I had never developed the skill of making friends, and I had no idea how to start a life.

I got an occasional letter from home and even a cassette tape with my mom singing a song talking about how much I was loved. I knew she meant it in her strange way, but I wasn't sure what to do with it.

One thing I knew for sure, and that was this: since I had been thrown out of my family, I was going to pursue the music that was in my heart.

I hadn't been able to do that before because of fear of rejection. But now that it was a full-fledged reality: I was free! Or, so I thought.

Chapter 38

# MARRIAGE #1

had been excommunicated from the church for having a relationship with a girl in Belgium. As I mentioned, she was one of several that I had flirted with, but the only one where I got myself in trouble.

I imagined that I loved her, really having no idea what that meant. I really think in retrospect that I was in love with the idea that someone thought I was so special when no one else had.

After a few months on my own, I saved some money and flew back to Belgium and married that girl that I had been with at the end of my mission. We really knew nothing about each other, and the likelihood of success of that marriage was small, particularly because I was so poorly prepared for life.

Of course, my mom advised against that, and she was right. But the reasons and the set-up was all wrong. I couldn't hear the counsel, knew I was personally rejected, and everything was aimed at my evil nature and sin.

Being completely unaware of my failings, depression, inability to cope and all that stuff I blissfully blasted forward. After all, I knew that "I was in control."

What I didn't know is that there were thousands of pounds of baggage I was carrying around that was going to wreck my life and hurt those around me again and again over the next decades.

I got promoted quickly at my job. I completed 30 months of training in 18. I was heavily involved in creating a music career for myself as well. I was in a band. I played local clubs and directed several community musicals. I was creating a local name for myself.

I was given an opportunity for a large promotion by moving down to San Francisco and I took it. At the same time I had my first son and life was moving right along.

I figured this utility job would be a summer job sort of thing at best and that within a few years I would be firmly and fully established as a musician.

My family continued to reject both of us, and when my little brother got married, we were allowed to attend the wedding reception, just barely, if we 'sat in the back, and weren't seen.' That is an exaggeration—but only slightly. Let me explain.

Because my mom had taught all of us music growing up, it was very common for our family to perform frequently at church functions, community events and professional venues.

So at the wedding reception everyone in the family was performing musically on stage as part of the program. I was informed that I was unworthy to perform in that capacity and would not be allowed to participate with the family on stage. Needless to say we didn't stay very long.

In a surprise twist, my family actually stopped by my house once on their way to summer vacation one year. They stayed for a few minutes and pretended to be interested in what we were doing. That was the only visit to my place. We lived an hour away.

I do remember one visit that we paid to my parent's house a few months after we had our first child. That would have been about 3½ years into our marriage.

I remember being severely chastised afterwards because my wife had not taken 'good enough' care of our baby and we were disgraceful in our behavior. Nothing remarkable had happened during the visit and I had no idea what my mother was talking about.

If I had been healthy, I would have realized that I was at a crossroads again. Cut the ties with the 'mom' and dump her from my life, or continue to grovel and scrape for my mom's approval.

Anybody with any brains or a healthy mind would have realized this was a time to make the cut. I did not even see that as an option. I just needed to be 'better' somehow, and everything would be OK.

I was too dependent on her approval to do that. My permanent conditioning of 'not being good enough,' and my desperation for her approval seemed to win every time. I couldn't cut the cords.

The success I had at work felt good but didn't count, because my whole life was out of bounds. The music success was real and growing, but 'evil.' The isolation and rejection was real and I quickly found myself floundering and lost. The supremacy of 'not being good enough' kicked in again.

# Chapter 39

# DIVORCE—THE SECOND CLIFF

The depression became worse and worse when I realize nothing I could do would ever satisfy my mom. I was in an endless loop of trying everything I could to get the approval of exactly those people who would never give me that approval.

My career moved quickly. The opportunities to direct musical theater in our town and neighboring communities increased. I was the musical director for several musicals, wrote and performed original music and appeared to be expanding.

I was active in volleyball on both the church and a community team because of the volleyball experience I'd had in college. From the outside, it would have appeared that everything was going as good as it could go.

So this strange combination led me to the following: I was happier than I ought to be with the successes of my own life. I was miserable beyond belief because I could never get the approval of my mom. I was depressed and hated and feared every day.

I was both past my upper limit of happiness (I didn't deserve this because I was evil) and depressed at my lack of ability to make progress 'back into the family,' or get recognition for the successes I was having.

Another recipe for a massive disaster. I cheated on my wife, trashed the relationship, burned everything to the ground and got fired from the job I was doing so well at. Self-sabotage, depression at its finest, and on my face I found myself once again.

In retrospect, it seems like I was certain that the God my mother taught me required that I be miserable and suffering at all times until I reached her approved level of behavior and achievement.

Of course, this is idiotic. No one, God or anyone else, trying to encourage and support the development of another, would go about it this way, but that was my reality.

# Chapter 40

# WHO CARES?

After the divorce, things got really ugly with my family. I was pretty much persona non grata. My younger brothers and sisters were pretty much completely poisoned by the attitude of my parents.

'I told you so' was the feeling and there was no doubt that my parents assumed, mostly my mom, that I was irrevocably doomed to a life in hell.

I had a new girlfriend for a while and she and I moved into an apartment together and then she and I separated and came back together three or four times as a reflection of the tumultuous nature of my own personal journey.

That entire saga lasted less than a year because I was personally in such bad shape. I started drinking again and using drugs.

I had several temporary jobs before a good friend of mine found me a job back in the utility industry in Arizona. It was an amazing gift and I was grateful. As karma would have it, I was able to return the favor some 20 years later.

I moved to Arizona. Partly because I felt guilty, partly because the divorce was not final even though we have been separated for a year and mostly so I could see my kids, I also moved my soon to be ex-wife as well.

She did not have a job at the time. In addition, because of my overpowering guilt, I kept thinking I should get back together with her. There is that 'should' again. I think she hoped that might happen, so she agreed to come.

Once in Arizona, I opened a recording studio to pursue the music more seriously. I started getting clients in my studio and session work at other studios around town.

I was an accomplished pianist, keyboard player, drum machine and synth programmer. This success felt really good, but was always tempered by the sure knowledge that it was evil.

I lived alone for a couple of years and focused on creating the musical career I wanted.

I started believing that maybe the whole set-up of my life was wrong. Maybe all this family and religion was wrong and not for me. Maybe I just couldn't do it.

But the context was always poison because it felt like 'maybe I'm not good enough to have this.' My depression never let me get objective enough to see what I truly wanted separate from early programming.

At first I felt satisfied living alone, but after a while, my unhealthy need for external approval drove me to look for some kind of relationship. In retrospect, I was desperate to mean something to somebody and was willing to do almost anything to get it.

I dated several girls but nothing lasted very long or meant anything. I'm sure I was quite incapable of anything meaningful, although I did not realize it at the time.

After a couple of years, I met another gal and strongly felt like I needed to have a relationship again to prove something to myself. While I did not think anything consciously, I wanted someone to fall for me and make me the most important person in their world.

The truth was far more deadly. I was killing all my feelings, and simply hiding the pain under alcohol, dating and the one bright spot—music.

# Chapter 41

# AROUND WE GO AGAIN

told myself that this time it would be different. After all, this woman had a significant background in music and she liked the fact that I was running a studio.

But in reality, I was thrashing about in a sea of pain and confusion. She had been raised in an abusive home, and had been promiscuous in her teen years as a result. She was at least as desperate for approval as I was, and I did not realize this. Even if I had known, I would not have known what it all meant.

I cheated on her regularly while we were dating. I did not even know what fidelity was. Everything about my life had been about hiding, getting away with what you could and lying to cover up.

I was pretending to be in love. She knew what was going on about the other women and ignored it because of her own insecurity and because I kept promising to do better.

Despite all the cheating, drinking and everything else and against anyone's intelligent judgement, we got married.

This was another mistake and in retrospect, with the benefit of 30 years of perspective, I realize I did not love this woman, and I didn't even actually know what love was. That is painful to admit at this point but I don't think I had ever experienced it for myself.

After the initial turmoil, things settled down and I make a commitment to myself to stay married. I promised myself and her that I would honor the relationship.

I promised myself at the same time that I would build up the studio and pursue the music and the career at the utility as fast and as hard as I could. The intention was still to build the music and dump the utility as soon as possible.

During the time we had been dating, I told her I was raised as a Mormon and told her about the church. She wanted to know more so I help her learn. She met with Mormon missionaries and was baptized into the church a few months before we got married.

Because of her baptism and my innate and unflagging need to get back in good with my family, this seemed like the perfect path. We started going to church, and unfortunately, this triggered an even bigger need for me to start on the 'approval' path with my mom.

Another element in the equation was my wife's family. My mother-in-law was a very sad person. She had lost the love of her life at a young age, and had been married for many years to an abusive and stingy man. She was bitter and jaded and was furious when we decided to have children.

This led me even more to want to create a relationship with my mom and family so that my wife would have some family who supported her. So again, everything on the line for external approval.

This whole approach was a monumental mistake. Let's just count the cards as they are right now. I jumped into a relationship for the wrong reasons. I did not know what love was.

I am knowingly pursuing a relationship with my mom, even though I know she hates my musical endeavors. I somehow think that all this will be OK, even though nothing has changed.

Still worse, I am blissfully unaware of the brokenness of my own behaviors. I have not done any work with myself to understand my dependence on approval from my mom.

I had no idea that everything I was doing was reactionary and from a place of bouncing in and out of being severely depressed. I just knew that for a moment, I felt relieved from the pain of self-loathing.

I was living in a place of not feeling, not even knowing that I was not feeling and looking all the time for external validation and approval to create a sense of being OK.

I wanted validation first from my mom, who disapproves of what I do, then from a relationship I don't feel anything in and eventually from the vindication of having a family and a successful career in a field I am not interested in. Being OK in my own skin wasn't even in the equation.

Don't get me wrong, being validated by your parents, your spouse, your work and other external sources is fine, but it only works if you have your head on right.

What I didn't know and couldn't know were two things. My new wife had been raised in an abusive home with a dad who was an alcoholic and a mom who told her early in her life she was not wanted. She was at least as broken as I was and I didn't even know it. Even if I had, I would have had no idea what to do about it.

Our marriage relationship was fairly flimsy from the start. In addition to the rocky start, everything shifted so that I was pursuing my mom's approval again. My wife latched on to that, and it soon became my wife and my mom against me.

I thought that if I got married, had kids, was active in the church and pursued making my mom happy that somehow life would take care of itself. Saying that now makes me realize what an idiot I was but that's what you do through the lens of depression.

It was clear from early in our relationship that Elizabeth had no idea how to raise children. I remember regularly getting phone calls at work with her in total panic. She would ask me to reprimand or discipline kids on the phone because she was completely incapable of handling these things.

For any sane person that would've been a warning sign, but I was too broken myself to pay attention. Besides, somehow I just knew that everything would take care of itself if I just learned to be like I was 'supposed to be' according to my mom.

I gave up the booze and drugs and started trying to get myself back in favor with my family and back in the church. I was caught between two feelings. I felt like the church doctrine was right and that I could actually find a home there.

On the other hand, I was trying everything just to get approval and was so caught up and broken that I could not pursue this for the right reasons.

I still could not get away from the feeling that the God I had been taught from my youth was a God of punishment and retribution. This meant I must be sad and miserable until I have achieved the status and recognition I am 'supposed' to have.

It was decades before I learned that my mom was not God, had no special connection to his ear and was subject to the same pains, sins, stupidity and need to change and grow as the rest of us.

Obvious from the outside and obvious in retrospect, but painfully hidden to a depressed soul stuck in the eternal certainty of 'never good enough.'

# Chapter 42

# DESTROY THE EVIDENCE

fter we had three children my mom started poisoning Elizabeth with the idea that my two children from my first marriage were old baggage and should not be permitted to interfere with my current life.

This led to one of the saddest and sorriest situations of my life and one of my deepest regrets.

In an earlier chapter I described my childhood ritual of going to my grandfather's farm in the summertime. That place in Wyoming had a very, very special place in my heart. It still does.

Because of this feeling, which was deep and powerful, I wanted to take my children there and have them experience that peace and beauty as well. I did not understand why it was so powerful for me. I have ideas now, but then, it was just the feeling.

It so happened that my parents had purchased the old homestead.

This meant my mom and dad now lived in the house my mother was born in, which was the very place I had gone each summer as a child. It was perfect, I could visit my parents and let my children see the beautiful farm and at the same time create some kind of relationship.

My mom had other ideas. She convinced my dad that the two children from my first marriage were dangerous and a threat to their financial future. I never understood the logic.

The story my mom told me was that she feared that if I brought my kids from my first marriage to visit, they would somehow get injured on the farm. Then their mother, my ex-wife, would sue them and ruin their financial future.

My first wife had never demonstrated any language or behavior at any time that would have created such a ridiculous impression. Nevertheless, my mom called me one day and told me they had decided I was not allowed to bring my first two children to visit the farm anymore.

I was totally brokenhearted and had no idea what to do. At first I just couldn't comprehend what she was telling me. I ask what else we could do to have them get to know their grandparents.

I was then further destroyed when she told me that she did not want to have a relationship with them at this time. Perhaps there would be some day in the future, when they were adults, for that to happen, but not now.

It was the most insane nonsense I had ever heard in my life. It was as if they were declared old baggage and unwanted refuse. I found myself in complete emotional meltdown with no idea what to do.

I could either continue the relationship with my family, which I craved at an unhealthy level or I could continue a relationship with the two children for my first marriage. To my shame and in a monument to depression and stupidity, I 'accepted the trade.'

Again, I was up against the wall. My depression and drive to be 'good enough' gave me the following twisted logic. 'If my mom thinks I should do this, then she must be right. I will pursue the relationship with my 'new kids' and my parents, and then the 'old kids' will get taken care of somehow, right? OK, if that's what it takes, let's go.'

I was wrong. It's a trade I would never make again and I have blamed myself and hated myself incessantly because of that insanity. Having thrown myself fully into the new relationship, I sort of took the position that I would "outperform" my mother's expectation in every respect.

I continued to see the two kids from my first marriage until their mother and her new husband moved away from Arizona. The visits were short and increasingly uncomfortable because my second wife had adopted my mother's rejection of them.

The bottom line was the cost of the relationship with my family was alienation from my two older children. That consequence and cost is something I have worked hard to rectify, but it still will require years of work.

# Chapter 43

# THE WRONG WALL

As I mentioned in a previous chapter, music was a big part of our family growing up. Well, If I was going to impress my mom, I better get busy. I taught my kids to sing, to play the piano and other instruments. I got involved in community work and in the neighborhood schools to help with their music and drama programs.

All good things to do, but the crazy driving force for me was just to do everything I could think of that would somehow create approval in my mom's mind.

The kids were good and impressive as performers in their growing up years. The 'old kids' were rejected by my mom, but the 'new kids' were allowed to the farm and in her life. Somehow that was all supposed to make everything 'okay.'

What madness had I created?

The pain was building inside of me. I had a weak and groundless relationship with my wife. I had a fake relationship with my parents based on alienating my two older children. I hated myself for that.

Center stage was the certainty that I was still not okay and the pain was building to a level of insanity.

It went on and on as I lived in a complete shambles of a life. I got promotions and more money. Everything looked okay from the outside.

Inside, my ability to feel became less and less. I looked outside for every cue about what I should be doing and how I should feel.

Suddenly, it seemed like I had begun getting approval from the very people I wanted.

As you would expect, it did not bring the satisfaction imagined. Almost nothing is as good as you think it's going to be, right?

As the old saying goes, I was at the top of a ladder on the wrong wall.

# Chapter 44

# SDLB

Those that do rehab work know what that stands for. It stands for 'self-defeating learned behaviors.' The problem was that I could not see what I was doing, and I had no external voice guiding me in my journey.

I had buried myself in self-sabotage so long I didn't know anything else. It was only a matter of time before my basket of depression exploded. Here are some examples.

I became convinced that if I got high enough up in my career and made enough money I would somehow be okay.

I was just certain, that if I had a whole bunch of kids and they were impressive, that must mean I'm okay, right?

I was trying to deal with the fact that my mom did not approve of a musical career. I wish I had told her to go to hell. But I was too weak and locked in the depression.

Any of this sound familiar?

Every time I talked about the studio it was not pleasant. No success that I had mattered. I had released several albums and was getting good airplay on Phoenix radio stations. So, what?

One summer, we went to the farm with the kids and I took two albums of original work that I had written and released. My mom wasn't interested and I don't remember that she even listened to any of the songs.

Only one person of the entire extended family listened to the music. My mom's sister. She took the time to listen, comment and ask questions. She still holds a very soft spot in my heart today because of that interest.

I had many opportunities to do volunteer work in the community and church. Most of this involved music. At church I began to become prominent fixture in musical circles, and was often asked to direct both our local and regional choirs.

We had several children at that point and my wife's time was largely taken up in looking after kids. She stopped working when we had children because she decided she wanted to. However, the choice was hollow and she developed a big resentment of my 'success and notoriety.'

This was odd, because the success was very localized in the community and church. Nevertheless, the negativity became palpable. In addition, the studio was taking more time and as it became more successful, I was essentially working two full-time jobs.

This was actually what we had intended, because we were preparing to go full time into the studio business and drop the 'summer job' at the utility. What I also didn't know was that she resented the fact that I had female clients in the studio.

It had never occurred to me that this was a problem. The studio was located in the house in additions we had made, so I never even thought about the jealousy thing.

I felt undermined and a disappearing support for the studio as a career. This came also because my wife adopted not only my mom's negativity toward the kids from my first marriage, but also toward my musical endeavors.

Music, the one big thing I thought we had in common, became a problem. Because of her own emotional issues and insecurity my wife needed to be visible and prominent in all the musical work I did in the community and church in order to feel ok.

As her own personality disorders were coming to the fore, I began to feel more and more distant from myself and my wife. Her ability to cope with kids and life became less and less.

My coping skills were abysmal and my ability to feel at all was fast disappearing. So things spiraled down from there.

Even my successes had become poison.

# Chapter 45

# PAVE OVER THE GRAVEYARD

W e came to a crucial decision point. I either needed to quit working at the utility and pursue the studio and the music career full-time, or close the studio and devote my attention and activity to the other career.

Again, my unhealthy need for approval and having no personal bearings destroyed any semblance of an intelligent decision-making process.

I literally lived for the approval of others, buried all the things I felt and assumed that my feelings and intuitions were wrong and that someone else was in possession of the 'right way.'

Previously, I mentioned that there was a decision regarding music that massively increased the depth and power of depression in my life. This decision was pivotal in shaping the next 20+ years. This was that decision.

Giving into the pressure from my mom, I closed the studio.

I basically abandoned my kids from my first marriage, I closed the studio because pursuing music was somehow wrong. I paved over everything that I thought was important and gave all the power to someone else. I burned in hell in my mind, but thought somehow I was finally on the right path.

All this really meant was that I paved over the first 37 years of my life and declared in all a failure. Nothing that I had wanted or created amounted to anything.

That was the feeling I had. I could not live with that feeling, so I turn off all my feelings, and from that time forward, I felt nothing.

Closing the studio was complicated. Because it was in the house, I couldn't sell it as a business. I was the sole engineer and creative producer, so I was the only talent. I had to close it down and go out of business.

Because it was so busy, the only way to close it down was to file bankruptcy. I did that too. Not a reorganization, but a liquidation, which was another devastating blow to both my self-esteem and my ability to cope.

Imagine how stupid. A successful career and a successful recording studio. And the only way forward is through bankruptcy? What utter madness is that?

That pivotal decision trashed the next two decades. Effectively what happened was that I lost every piece of myself I thought was valuable.

In retrospect the choice that I made was to pursue validation from my mom at the expense of declaring my older two kids unimportant, the music career that I wanted to pursue evil, and everything that I had valued in life up to that point was not worthy and not significant.

Stated in that bold and ugly way it was a decision of utter madness and could only be fueled by depression and desperation. Nothing else accounts for such insanity.

At the time I was so desperate for the approval I could not see anything else. The depression had taken me to a place where the only thing that mattered was the approval of my parents.

Many times during this journey I wondered what death would feel like. I never actually made elaborate suicide plans, but the thought of leaving the madness was not strange and certainly did not seem repulsive.

It often occurred to me that perhaps everyone in this circumstance would be far better off if I were not there. The decisions I had made seem to ruin everyone else's life. And there were a number of times when I considered the final question.

Nevertheless, I had made a decision to throw away everything I had ever wanted to be and pursue a career in electricity which did not interest me in the least. I happened to be really good at it, intuitively knowing things that sometimes took others years to figure out.

Success was easy.

Kill my feelings and Play the game.

# Chapter 46

# MASKING THE PAIN

T he emotional pain was relentless and intense. Sometimes I just wanted it all to end so badly I considered just running away and vanishing. Go where? Do what? Who cares?

I tried to make up for it in many ways. One was music. Something that was fun and that provided temporary relief was directing choirs, orchestras and other musical or dramatic groups.

This was fun because it was a huge joy for me to get great performances out of people who didn't feel like they had talent. Essentially, I loved to help people do things they didn't believe they could do.

Taking a band of essentially untrained volunteers, teaching them four-part choral harmony and then helping them perform to a standard beyond their wildest expectation was absolute pleasure.

It's interesting, because that feeling, that desire to help people do things they consider impossible is what drives me today in the work that I do now.

My greatest fulfillment comes in helping people overcome enormous challenges and create results they might feel are 'impossible.'

That drive helped me become extremely successful in the electricity industry. I was willing to take on projects that seemed doomed or beset with insurmountable obstacles others would avoid.

A second distraction was to bury myself in my work.

Promotions moved us from Arizona to Idaho. I became prominent first in statewide, then regional and ultimately national groups that create and control standards of governance and rulemaking for the electric power industry.

De-regulation was becoming fashionable at this point and so much of the work that I did for various utilities involved creation and implementation of new schemes.

The federal government was anxious to make changes in how utilities ran their grid. My natural talent at getting difficult things created opportunities for leadership positions all over the industry.

Career success came quickly and in great abundance. My feelings remained dead and my personal life remained empty and hollow.

It was obvious, even to my wife that I was miserable and floundering. It was out habit to take early morning walks before work. Frequently our discussions were about 'what was wrong with me?'

I did not know and could not answer the questions. I only knew that I was possessed of a vague unhappiness and a relentless longing for something I could not define. My feelings were so disconnected from my reality that I had no frame of reference to begin discussions.

The other problem was I was gone so much there was very little opportunity to conduct any meaningful assessment of what was wrong and what to do about it.

So the conversations were fruitless, and I powered off to bury myself in work and create the results I was good at and now was becoming famous for.

I was totally lost in deep depression at this point. I had never created a solid foundation for personal relationships. That fact was a massive block to success

The fact that she had been raised in a way that left her completely broken made this a situation where neither one of us had the capability to understand what was happening or the knowledge or skill to address the problem.

Chapter 47

# THE BIG MOUNTAIN

O pportunities continued to come in rapid succession. In a few years we
ended up in California. I was in a leadership position in a new organization
that was charting new territory for the electric industry.

A startup company is particularly stressful, even for the most stable
relationships. Since our relationship was anything but stable and healthy, adding
the stresses and demands of a start-up company to an already fragile situation
initiated a slow motion dance of death.

The workload was insane and initially we worked seven days a week,
sometimes 16 hours a day. In addition there was a great deal of travel involved,
which meant I was home even less than I had been in the previous job.

That kind of schedule took its toll on relationships all over the organization.
Mine wasn't the only one in trouble. I have often reflected since then at this
ridiculous cost of 'progress.' Even given the amazing things we did in the 'work'
arena, is the human cost worth it? A discussion for another day.

After he start-up phase, the intensity and demand of the job diminished only
slightly. I rose up through the ranks quickly and became a manager, then the
director and ultimately a C-level executive.

I had achieved prominence locally and nationally in the industry and was
making plenty of money. We had a big house, lots of cars, and all the trappings
that made a "great success."

You would think that this would be a 'happy' place, right?

Not really. This is actually where the terror starts. As the dust settles, I'm a very high-ranking executive in a career I don't care about and everything that I wanted to do is absent from my life.

I was a miserable absentee workaholic, with no feelings and living in fear because I knew for sure I was "not good enough." Elizabeth was a clinging wreck with too many kids at home, not enough help and frantic that I would leave her.

There was no love or feeling in our relationship. But I had no intention of leaving or anything of the kind. I had already traded everything I wanted for this mess, and feelings or no feelings, I was not intending to give it up.

With all this success, I had achieved "approval" from my family, and we were welcomed at all family gatherings. I had returned to activity and even had "positions" in our church. We had eight beautiful children and all of them were healthy. What else could be better?

But things were way past my ability to control.

There is a book titled "I Hate You, Don't Leave Me." It is a book that describes the behaviors and characteristics of the "borderline personality disorder."

My wife's behaviors matched the descriptions in that book exactly. As it turns out, in our later divorce and custody battles, which are coming in the next chapters, her personality tests suggested she had this condition.

I had not seen the book at that time, or sought any help for myself from any book or counselor that might help us deal with our struggles.

In my universe, depression, borderline personality disorder or other mental illness was something 'other people' dealt with, and certainly not something I needed to even think about.

I just figured this was how it was, and I would stumble through. I had what I wanted, or thought I wanted, and all this pain was just the cost.

Of course, it doesn't work that way. I imagine that it would have been like a movie where you in the audience can see something coming that the players in the movie don't know. Destruction was just around the corner.

I traveled a lot. I was often away for 3 or 4 days at a time on business to cities all over the US and Canada. Consistent with the fears of the borderline personality, my wife was in a constant state of fear that somehow I was having affairs.

I did not drink, fool around, or pursue anything outside of our marriage. We were married 16 years. I did, on occasion, go to a nightclub, cabaret or strip club when on these business trips.

I knew this made her angry, and repeatedly lied about it and then promised not to do it again. However, when I was away, the loneliness and emptiness inside plus the lack of any real relationship with her won the day.

So by this time you can see the size of the play. On the outside everything was fine. I had achieved national prominence in my employment. I was making significant amounts of money and afforded all of us a very comfortable lifestyle. My family has taken us in as 'all healed' and 'all is well.'

And the earthquake is coming.

# Chapter 48

# THE OTHER SHOE

There were three things wrong with this picture. I was only vaguely aware of the depth of the issues and blissfully lived in a state of denial and struggle with my own demons. It was only a matter of time before a spectacular crash came.

First of all, my wife was miserable. I sensed this, but I did not know what to do. I did nothing to address this, and I did not know how. She had no interest in the relationship and often considered herself isolated and lonely.

She was not taking care of the children. I was gone so much I did not know. Often, she would lock herself in the study and the kids would do whatever they wanted when they came home from school. I didn't know any of this until the court battles during the divorce.

The second thing was that I was totally miserable. In an effort to achieve the approval I craved, I had 'paved over' every piece of my life I thought was important and had declared it all unworthy.

I had done this so that I could get the 'blessing' of my mother, which was an unhealthy obsession I had left over from the abusive childhood. The approval came, but brought no peace.

The third was that I was working all the time, and was rarely home. This left me unaware of how bad things were at home. As a parent, it is my responsibility to know, and I failed. I was depressed and angry with myself for my inability to somehow 'fix' the situation.

The saddest thing is that instead of doing something, I merely hoped everything was OK, and assumed if I just kept pushing forward that somehow it would all work out.

I was so depressed I was unable to see any way to deal with any of this. I often would spend hours strategizing and thinking how I might make something better in our relationship.

I remember like yesterday the night that it all came down.

It was my wife's birthday. I had planned an elaborate celebration, shopping, dinner and everything else I could think of. At the end of the night, when we drove home in a luxury car to our 5600 square-foot five-acre mansion, it happened.

As we pulled in the driveway at about 11:30pm, she got angry with me and started yelling. At first I had no idea what was wrong. After a time, the only thing I understood was that I had ended the evening too early and that was simply inexcusable.

I was lost. I was truly and completely and utterly lost and dumbfounded. I had no idea what to say, think or do. At first I participated in the argument and then I simply collapsed.

Once again, I knew that nothing I could possibly do would be right. It was the Gordian knot. The mystical magical not that cannot be unraveled. It knew for certain that I did not have the capacity to solve the puzzle and the vortex of confusion and pain went over my head.

The argument lasted for an hour or so. No one had been drinking because we did not drink. It was all emotional intoxication and madness.

We had been married over 16 years and I felt like I did not recognize this person was I was looking at. I had no idea what to do to fix the situation and I had no idea how to move forward.

I was an empty well, with no reserve to draw on. The bottom line was that I had given up everything I wanted for this, and it too was failing and failing badly.

After this disaster, I lost all interest and was totally disengaged. I was a failure at a relationship again, and I didn't know what to do.

I had never had a true confidant in my life, so I had no one to talk to. I was lost and had nowhere to turn, and I began the familiar cycle of self-loathing again.

I withdrew and sunk deeper and deeper inside myself. Only at work was I able to summon any direction, although one of the other executives said I seemed really out of sorts. No kidding…

I was desperate for some release and someone to talk to. I tried the counselor at work, but I didn't dare be honest about my troubles at home, because I was worried about the effect on my job.

My mom was out of the question, so I kept it all inside, as I always did, and the depressive spiral got deeper and deeper.

I tried over and over again to broach the subject with my wife, and to describe how disconnected I was. It only caused fights, and more distance. I struggled for some time, and finally I resigned myself to permanent misery.

# Chapter 49

# THE OTHER 'OTHER SHOE'

A few months before this personal apocalypse, they had hired another vice-president at work who was a single woman. She already had a reputation for chasing and having affairs with married men, but I didn't know it. I never paid attention to office gossip.

It was a high stress time in the organization and there was a lot going on. The CEO had asked me to help this woman to get familiar with the company priorities and procedures and to help her come on board successfully.

Frequent meetings turned to interest and I began down the slippery slope of seeing 'the other woman.' I knew this would ruin everything in my life, but I could not see now anything could be more terrible than it already was.

I wanted to die already, and felt like nothing mattered anyway, so who cares?

It's probably important to note that up to that time, there had never been a spark of interest in another woman outside my marriage.

I had considered suicide, but not another woman. This had simply not been part of the equation. Things progressed over several months, we started having an affair and as it always does, it came out.

I separated from my wife, moved into an apartment and then eventually in with 'the other woman.'

The new relationship was a bad idea from the start. My whole life was on fire and I had no idea what to do about it. This temporary refuge was simply a place to hide.

But I did not have either the wisdom or the emotional strength to recognize how foolish such a course of action was. I was fleeing the misery of the current situation and took no thought for the intelligence of the destination.

I did know that I hated everything in my life. I remember actually hiding in the new house I was living in and silently screaming 'I don't want to be here.'

Screaming silently at the top of my lungs. Screaming so hard that if it had been out loud everyone in the neighborhood would have heard my voice. That was the intensity of that primal cry for help.

I was slowly falling completely and absolutely apart.

In this new relationship I was reintroduced to alcohol. I had been completely dry for 16 years and so this was new all over again.

This woman had a habit of drinking every day, and it became common practice to stop every day on the way home from work and have at least a couple of martinis.

Since I had never really done any social drinking in my life, I had no idea what appropriate social drinking looked like. So I moved from being clean and sober to drinking every day over a period of probably two weeks.

That should've been the first warning sign, but I was too glad to be out of the other misery to pay attention. Besides, the drinking provided a welcome relief and a new way to hide from the sadness and terror still raging inside.

As the news of my choices spread among my family, the effects were predictable and fierce. No surprises here. The consequences were immediate and total banishment from my family, my church, and everyone I knew in my personal life.

I was now alone, with this new woman as my sole companion. This change brought overflowing guilt which sent me spiraling down into deeper and deeper depression. Not surprisingly, the alcohol became a welcome numbing relief.

We partied hard, took vacations all over the place and basically did everything humanly possible to pretend that life was grand. Within a few months my new girlfriend got fired from her executive position at work and struggled for months to find a job.

Things were getting really scary.

Those who have depression or those who live with a depressed person know that alcohol and drugs are frequent choices to hide the pain.

When blackness is all you can see, almost any form of relief is better than the terrifying hole in your mind. The drugs make you numb.

Without the numbing, there is nothing to keep you from the abyss.

It has no name, there is no description, and I simply call it 'The Name Of The Black.'

# Chapter 50

# 34 STORIES TO THE PAVEMENT

did everything I could to maintain control and a good face at work, and I was mostly successful. However, my personal problems soon became public gossip, and there I was having discussions with the CEO about how to handle the fallout.

The CEO was ecstatic about my plight and clearly enjoyed the situation. There was lots of sympathetic posturing, but it was clear what was going on in his mind.

He and I had disagreed on several critical issues in previous months and occasionally the board had overruled his choices and insisted he make decisions consistent with my advice.

He was the CEO and I was second-in-command so generally the decisions were his to make and mine to advise. I made my advice and reasoning clear, but after the decisions, I never undermined the path forward. But that did not lessen the acrimony he felt at having lost some battles.

In addition, he did not like the national prominence and attention that had been paid to me during the formation of the company.

My personal turmoil presented an opportunity to solve this inconvenience.

About a year went by in this difficult work situation. It became increasingly obvious that the CEO was trying to structure things to 'help' me leave the company so that I would no longer be a thorn in his side.

Ultimately, it seemed to me that leaving was probably for the best.

I had achieved national prominence and I knew that there would be something else I could do without too much trouble. Six months before the turmoil started I had already had two other job offers.

I considered leaving at that time but the chairman of the Board of Directors asked me to stay, again against the wishes of the CEO. That had really irritated the CEO since they had gone around him again.

I left and immediately got a private consulting contract making even more money. The money was never the problem.

# Chapter 51

# DIVORCE AGAIN AND WORSE

ivorce proceedings were well underway by this time and in the middle everything took a gigantic turn for the worse. What could have been a simple divorce with mediation and some property settlement suddenly became a monumental mess.

My soon-to-be ex-wife falsely accused me of all kinds of abuse in order to gain control of the children.

From out of nowhere, State agencies, Child protective services, counselors, psychologists, court-appointed advocates and a host of others immediately became part of my life for the next 18 months.

Suddenly, nothing mattered except stabilizing my life, taking care of my kids and trying to have some semblance of a life back.

My first reaction would be to say that this 18 month period was the worst nightmare of my whole life. Truthfully, I had so many nightmare periods that all I can really say is that it was one of the worst.

Something positive that came from this stressful time was that I got focused and had something to do besides wish I was dead.

A real downside of this torture cycle was that during the lengthy proceedings there are often long weeks of waiting.

During those times, I buried myself in alcohol and soon began drinking excessively. There was no end of blaming myself even though I had nothing to do with the accusations.

I had endless nightmares both during the night and awake blaming myself for the entire mess. What should I have done differently and what was I supposed to do now?

Psychology tests, polygraph tests, attorneys, counselors, child welfare services, CASA advocates, mediators and all of the peripheral agencies were involved in my life nearly every day. I learned a whole new lexicon as I waded through this mess.

It was obvious to me that because I was the man, there was an immediate assumption of guilt and the child welfare services people treated me like I was dead already.

It would be easy to assume that my point of view about the child protective services is biased. Fortunately, at the end of the preceding, CPS was reprimanded in court and ordered to completely modify the way they handled cases in the future.

The order was severe and actually shouted from the bench by a red-faced judge because of the obvious and blatant bias with which their proceedings had been handled.

It's going to sound like a screenplay concocted in the imagination of some fanciful writer, but what I am about to tell you is true.

After a lengthy battle where child welfare services did everything possible to prove my guilt, I was exonerated of all charges. The psychologist who my wife used was banned in perpetuity from practicing in that jurisdiction for lying in court.

CPS was severely reprimanded for bias and ordered to overhaul their entire procedure manual consistent with the orders of the trial.

I was awarded sole legal and physical custody of all the children, and my now ex-wife was denied permission for visitations overnight, because of her inability to manage the kids.

The battle was over. The wounded were everywhere. The battlefield was bloody. The innocent had been victimized, particularly the children.

I had all the kids.

I was in a new relationship that never should have been started in the first place.

We did not live happily ever after.

## Chapter 52

# LET'S GET MARRIED AGAIN—SHALL WE?

The divorce was final nine months before the final custody orders were written. Even though I knew it was a bad idea, for some reason I married the woman I had an affair with. This would be my third marriage if you're counting.

As I mentioned, most of our relationship was based on partying and vacations because the money was plentiful and while you're partying it's easy to get disconnected from reality.

After the wedding, I learned that I was not the first married man she had wooed. I also learned that this was her third marriage as well, with a few failed 'live-in' relationships as well. It sounded just like me. We often joked about that, only it's not really funny.

This marriage was a move of desperation fueled by depression. I had been unhappy in that new situation from the first week. My silent screaming was real, and I knew it was not workable.

In hindsight, which is always 20/20, it was an obvious rebound move driven by my severe depression.

Both my second and my third wives had histories of mental illness in their families. My second wife was raised by an abusive alcoholic father and the mom who didn't want her.

My third wife had a suicide in her family. Her mom committed suicide when was nine and she was lied to for 12 years about what had happened.

When she was 21, things became so awkward in her family that she was finally told the truth.

She raged against her father for years and has never gotten over the abandonment or learned how to truly love for fear of loss.

From the vantage point of 14 years later, it's easy to see that now, and it's easy to say that now. At the time, everything I was doing was clouded by my own depression and self-loathing.

I felt a huge obligation and guilt concerning the kids. I knew I had failed them. I knew I had rescued them. But I did not know how to proceed effectively.

Both the past consequences and madness yet to come driven by my depression affect me, my kids and our relationship to this day.

The only thing that was plentifully abundant was money.

I had been able to keep high paying jobs all this time, and this was an easy way to continue to camouflage the problems and pretend them away. It will come as no surprise that this is not the key ingredient for success.

# Chapter 53

# HUMPTY DUMPTY OR HOW MANY WAYS CAN YOU CRACK AN EGG?

A bout 18 months pass with nothing changing. When this happens, for me at least I get the impression that "this is how life should be." "This is as good as it gets, so you better enjoy it."

There is always an underlying feeling of sadness, a certainty of inadequacy and a degree of comfort that the mask and barriers are keeping the demons at bay.

The next wrinkle in the story unfolds with a new job in a new place. After completing the contract I got after leaving my previous employer, I found an opportunity to interview for a job in Canada, still working in the industry in my area of expertise.

I left California, moved to Canada with all my children. Life was in a period of stasis, with the underlying sadness and inadequacy masked by settling in after the 'war' was over, vacations, excess money and constant hoopla.

I had been married two years at this point, and we were already having significant trouble. I knew this was a rebound relationship and was on a weak foundation from the start. But there were so many diversions, there was no time to pay attention to the basic truth.

The first two years of marriage had been completely absorbed with custody battles, settling the dust and barely beginning to create a 'post traumatic' life. Then my contract ended and I got a new job which required the enormous upheaval of moving to a new country.

It was a relationship I knew from the start was a poor choice. I chose to ignore all the warning signs and kept telling myself somehow things would be okay. After all, it seemed like somehow it could all settle down, right?

This was ignoring the obvious. I had already begun to drink excessively and I knew instinctively that somehow this was a Band-Aid and only a delay in an inevitable major shift that needed to take place in my life.

It's sad, because by this point I had abandoned all hope of creating a legacy in the area of my true passion, which was using music while helping others maximize their gifts and talents.

I also think that I was struggling with the trauma of having been accused of abusing my children. Even though I was completely vindicated, this accusation played on the fears of my childhood and magnified the mountain of uncertainty in me about being inadequate.

The pain and yearning was not gone, it was simply buried in a new job and alcohol. The only way I was able to manifest some form of excellence was in creating extraordinary results in the position I had been hired.

Creating those kind of results came from two places. I had natural gifts and talents that let me excel and also I was still driven by the terror of inadequacy and 'not being good enough' which drove me always to be an overachiever.

The job that I was hired to do was going well. Because I was in the same industry, I still got regular reports about what was going on in California.

About a year after I got to Canada, I found out something that provided some level of 'vindication.' The three executives who had pushed so hard for my "exit," from the previous job, had all been fired by the Board of Directors a few months earlier.

At my exit interview I had told the board of directors that they would let these three specific people go when they understood the truth of what was going on. They passed it off as the ravings of a disgruntled loser. Bittersweet news, at best.

The job situation in Canada came with some significant challenges. My work was in one city and my wife wanted to live in a different city 180 miles away. She thought her chances of getting work were far better in that city and her brother lived there.

This meant I was commuting 180 miles one way to work and consequently had a house in both cities. This led to my excessive absence from home, which was setting the stage for excessive isolation, disconnection from my kids and a repetition of the previous patterns.

I still didn't know at this point I was severely depressed and so I just decided to suck it up and make a go of it. Not surprisingly, I began to feel isolated and more depressed and disconnected from my family. This feeling of isolation grew more and more profound as the months went by.

Thinking about it now, the growing isolation from my kids added to the fact that I felt guilty about what they had been through before, with all the state agencies, through no fault of their own, but because of the lies of their mom.

My marriage relationship was empty. I am quite certain that I was not much of a marriage partner and the relationship was not rewarding for me either.

It was somewhat stable for the children, although my wife's resentment of my absence was growing quickly, even though when we moved we were both aware of how the situation would be while I had that job. In addition, it was her choice to live in the distant city.

It seemed okay conceptually, but in practice was virtually impossible to make work. By the time we had been there 18 months, things began to unravel.

I was drinking heavily and had begun using cocaine and other numbing drugs. I began having an affair with the secretary in my office just because the opportunity presented itself.

I knew everything was wrong and I knew it was going to hit the fan.

And I didn't know how to fix it.

# Chapter 54

# I KNOW SOMETHING IS WRONG

began to realize something was seriously wrong. I talked to my wife about possibly suffering from depression and she told me to go see the doctor. By this time our relationship struggles had become serious enough that she no longer cared what happened.

Because of my poorly developed support network with no friends, I had no one to talk to. My wife was alienated and I had no confidant.

I went to a doctor at the time and broached the subject He gave me some antidepressant pills, which made me sleepy and didn't seem to do much else. Because of my significant substance abuse the doctor was reluctant to do anything more significant. I quit taking them.

I should have started to see a counselor at that time, but I had neither the courage nor the inclination to do that. I was still convinced that seeing a counselor meant I was weak. Above all I could not validate the feeling of 'not being good enough.'

I created a Catch-22 situation where the substance abuse was getting in the way of potential diagnosis and treatment, and the depression itself was leading to repeated episodes of substance abuse to numb the emptiness and disconnection I felt from my life.

It's interesting how having too much money often delays making changes. You somehow get the false notion that enough money can fix anything. Let me tell you now once and for all, money is not the answer.

Money is not happiness. Money does not fix emptiness, depression and misery. Money does not by intimacy, trust, love or any of the essential human emotional needs. Those that believe otherwise are simply those who have not experienced money and think somehow that it will fix problems.

Money just keeps things temporarily at bay.

I stopped caring about what was going on around me. Thoughts of death and dying occurred more frequently, and the strain on the relationship became insane.

We separated only five years into the relationship. I was not surprised. In fact, it was really a self-fulfilling prophecy. What I really thought was 'I knew it.' By this time I had become completely convinced that I had no hope of a normal life or a stable situation.

The fact that I was failing at a third marriage, combined with the certainty that 'everything was always my fault' made me drown in hopelessness.

My wife was so angry that she was completely willing to let me have all the responsibility for failure, even though she knew we had experienced serious problems from the beginning.

I had no one to talk to and did not have the sense or the will to simply call a halt and get some help.

One of the significant signs of depression is reckless behavior. In thinking about and writing about that situation now I realize that I engaged in that type of behavior consistently.

Let me give you some examples. I loved fast cars. More horsepower and more speed was an exhilaration that was effective in masking pain just like the drugs.

One example is driving for an hour on a winding road, pedal all the way to the floor just to see if I could do it. Another example is driving 180 miles an hour for stretches of freeway just to see if I could get away with it and not die.

Wild combinations and overdoses of drugs were common. Reckless and promiscuous sexual behavior. Extreme risks all alone on lonely and out of bounds ski slopes. Those are just examples of many kinds of risky behavior.

All these resulted in warning signs, injuries and near disasters but no hospitalization or death. I just kept pushing the envelope without stopping.

## Chapter 55

# ANOTHER ONE BITES THE DUST

F lippant title. Given the empty state of my emotional life, and the disaster around me, it just seemed like that's just how it goes.

I assumed that my wife and I would divorce and she would go find some other prominent and wealthy executive to seduce.

After the separation, four of the children came to live with me. They all knew that I was drinking too much and knew that I was using some kind of drugs.

They knew that my life was a shambles but they would not live with my wife because she had abused them verbally and emotionally.

Because of her fear of abandonment and need for extreme control, either you were totally on her side and saluted to everything she needed or she excluded you and showered you with emotional exclusion and cruelty.

I really intended to be a good dad. I organized household chores. I organized two nights a week when we had dinner together. I tried to create some traditions. I made sure the kids got to school and I tried to supervise homework.

I actually think I did a really lousy job. There was all kinds of stuff going on under my nose that I didn't spot. Probably because of my own self-absorption and brokenness.

They lied all the time about where they had been and what they were doing. I found myself on the receiving end of all kinds of surprises. They stole credit cards and money and whatever else they could get their hands on.

Occasionally, I tried to have conversations about their lives and feelings. I wasn't very good at it and so not much real exchange took place. They patiently endured the attempts and then went about their way.

I didn't want to involve them in any of my problems because after all, they were children and should not be involved in my problems. Silly reasoning since they were involved anyway, by default.

So we ended up with this somewhat farcical situation where they knew I was using drugs, I denied it and was too proud and scared to get help.

They lied to me regularly about what they were doing in the house and out of the house and we just cruised along with a sort of unspoken mutual agreement to pretend.

Not understanding the nature of depression, it was genuinely baffling to me why I could be so successful career wise and financially and at the same time such an abysmal failure at both relationships, being a parent and being able to lead a 'normal' happy life.

One thing I remember during this period is that I reflected often that I seemed to feel nothing. I did not know what it was like to have real feelings.

I could play any role easily and adopt the behaviors appropriate with that situation, but my feelings had become so used to being numb and ignored that they played very little role in my daily life.

Every week I would make a new determination to do something better, create more family time, ask more questions, be more present and make changes to the pain.

It just never happened.

All my feelings were gone, except an overpowering sadness, an overpowering loneliness, a sick realization that I was failing as a dad and an overpowering certainty that I truly had no value.

I had become the self-fulfilling prophecy that I was 'not good enough.' Since I amounted to nothing, I sometimes entertained a question about what it would be like simply to be dead.

Chapter 56

# REASON TO LIVE?

M y habit had been to continually pretend that everything was okay. So that's what I did, full speed ahead. I went to work. They went to school or pretended to go to school. We went shopping on the weekends. We mowed the lawn, we cleaned the house. We went skiing in the winter.

The truth was that I was just going through the motions, day after day. The only thing keeping me functioning at all was the fact that I had four children living with me and I needed to provide for them.

Underneath the façade and the empty motions the truth was that even though all the physical things were taking care of, emotionally and spiritually the atmosphere was bankrupt. I tried to make up for it by shopping and buying clothes or music or movies. But it was all empty.

Every teenager goes through a period of rebellion, as a normal part of growing up. Getting away with things and hiding stuff from your parents is standard fare.

Because I was alone, gone too much and broken myself, the true parenting was not up to snuff. The outcome was that for these four teenagers those teen years wandered way, way outside the boundaries.

They had friends over all the time, and overnighters with any number of people were common. I tried to manage with some degree of supervision but the truth is they and their friends were drinking and using other substances on a regular basis.

I knew it was happening and didn't really know how to fix it. It is embarrassing to look back now and see the level of my own dysfunction and consequently the poor atmosphere that I provided for them to blossom and grow.

Two of the kids finished high school with fairly high marks and the opportunity to go to further schooling if they chose. One went on to university.

The other two dropped out of school and still haven't finished. I blame myself entirely for that and of course, blame myself for everything that went wrong. Cognitively, I realize that as adults they have choices but my default is always been to take responsibility for everything.

With the failure of my third marriage on the table, and divorce imminent, I began seriously wondering about whether or not life is worthwhile. After all, what was a really contributing in a positive way to anyone's life?

I wondered if everyone would be better off if I was gone. My soon-to-be ex-wife sensed my despair and actively tried to encourage me to commit suicide.

She often spoke of wishing I didn't exist or would somehow vanish. The favorite phrase I remember from her was "I keep wishing I could wake up in a world without you."

Perhaps the suicide of her mother when she was young played a role in those feelings, I can never know for sure. I do know it took years for her to get over her anger towards her dad and that she exhibited many behaviors of someone suffering from abandonment and attachment disorders.

The three girls that lived with my wife came to visit on weekends. I tried to make those visits interesting and fun, but I am sure that I failed. My wife spared no effort in poisoning the girls against me and in creating rumors and fear mongering.

The saddest but funniest incident I remember is the youngest girl who was 11 at the time became convinced by my wife that she was in danger because I had display swords hanging on the wall. These were oriental in design and came from my longtime involvement in martial arts.

These swords were not sharp and were for display purposes only. However my daughter exclaimed that she had dropped an apple and it had become impaled on a sword and therefore she was afraid for her life.

This, of course, was impossible since the swords pointed down and were flush with the wall.

This is simply an example of the paranoia rampant in the poisoned atmosphere.

# Chapter 57
# NOWHERE TO TURN

When marriage relationships crumble, and other bad things happen in life, people often turn to their family of origin for help and support. This might involve just emotional encouragement or it might involve financial support like a place to live or some money to get started over.

I haven't talked much about my family of origin during this part of the journey because there isn't anything to tell except bad news.

As soon as the 'other woman' showed up, as far as they were concerned, I was 'off the rails.' I might as well have been banished to the dark side of the moon.

I was persona non grata once again. Other than the occasional card, which did nothing but preach repentance to a damned soul, I was removed from the "family Christmas gift" rotation and contact was nonexistent or spotty.

I used to assume it was because nobody knew what to say and probably they were busy with their own lives. In reality, that was just excuses I made for the lack of love evidenced by my family of origin.

If someone you love is struggling, you reach out and see what you can do to help. Not just once, but as often as you can. And you don't quit. At least that's how I imagine things.

But to be truthful, I don't really know the reasons. I would be making up reasons if I put them here. What I knew was that I had no one to talk to, no one to turn to and that I was fully isolated.

A sad companion truth is that I had never learned how to create friendships, so I had nothing to turn to here and didn't know how to remedy that.

I had never learned how to give or receive love, and certainly didn't know to how to behave when everyone I thought should care about me didn't.

The way that we were raised as kids created isolation among most of my brothers and sisters. Other than periodic visits, real involvement in anyone else's life is nonexistent among all the siblings.

To this day, very little is shared between the siblings about what's going on in their lives. I'm not sure how that came about, but it's true.

The descent into the maelstrom continued, and with the overriding certainty that I was fundamentally flawed, I spiraled deeper into depression and the substance abuse became more and more profound.

I knew that I was spiraling toward destruction and death but I wasn't sure what to do about it and certainly didn't know how to stop it.

Of greater concern was that I was not sure I wanted to.

It got to the point where I drank heavily every night after work, and augmented this with other substances when they were available. I lived in two states, at work, and numb.

Obviously, this affected my focus and ability to do anything well. I'm sure people at work wondered what was wrong. I know they knew that something was out of order. Nobody ever said anything, but I suspected that it was a common gossip topic in the office.

# Chapter 58

# TRYING TO DIE

O n some weekends, the craziness wandered somewhere between severe and wildly out of control. To this day I am not able to understand why some of the things that happened didn't end up in death.

I totally wrecked the exotic sports car I had. Not being satisfied with its already prodigious performance, I had added parts and had it tuned until the tests showed north of 850 hp.

In one of the most vivid demonstrations of both stupidity and divine intervention, the final crash where I totaled the car ended with a tree branch ¼" inch from my eye when the car came to rest.

I walked away without a scratch. But a tiny ¼ inch difference separated me from certain death with a large tree branch slammed inside my brain.

I badly dislocated my shoulder on the ski slopes while skiing far too fast and on slopes I had no business being on. At another time I dislocated my knee so badly that it was 3 inches from where it should.

I didn't have it looked after, I simply skied down the slope on one leg, smashed it in place on the gondola on the way down and limped for a few days while it became tolerable. I let it heal on its own.

Nearly every weekend I increased the amount and combination of drugs I used until I was unconscious. I was hallucinating regularly and once cut up my mattress because I knew for sure someone was stuck inside.

Finally the physical pains in different parts of my body started to accumulate. I had some x-rays done. The news was predictable and bad. The accumulated damage over the years was extensive and there was nothing really that could be done.

Miraculously, today I am in good physical condition and I have no mobility limitations. But that miracle comes a little bit later in the story.

We have now come full circle. This is the time where the story in the prologue of this book took place. One of the serious binges found me face down on the floor having the conversation with myself I described.

I was completely lost, my head and my heart were helpless and hopeless and I could not even pretend to answer the question 'What do I do now?' I did not understand how I got where I was in my life, and I had no clue about finding a way out.

Chapter 59

# THE PERFECT STORM

could feel it in the air. I knew that something was coming to a head and would soon happen. It's like one of those movies where you see the terrible storm clouds on the north and on the west and on the east, and you know that the mighty upheaval is at hand.

I really expected that I would die. I thought that was what was coming. My soul was in constant turmoil and I began to feel a sense of impending fear and doom.

Everyone in the house seemed unusually alert and a bit on edge. There was nothing specific that was going on, there was just something at the verge.

About two weeks after the incident described in the last chapter, things started to happen. I have no explanation for some of these things, I simply present them as they occurred.

An accident occurred that put my 14-year-old son in the hospital. He and some friends had been playing with gasoline with the idea of making Molotov cocktails.

An accident ensued and he was badly burned. The burns were bad enough that he needed some skin grafts and so he was in a local hospital still recovering.

I was feeling awful about that accident. I assumed that somehow those burns were my fault. Not because I don't understand that teenage boys play with those kinds of things, I had myself played with explosives in high school.

But somehow I felt like if I had been more active, if I had been more present and paying attention to what was going on in his life, perhaps it would not have happened.

For those who don't believe in a God, or a God who cares about us, some of what follows here may seem absurd or so much nonsense. It doesn't really matter, because it represents a true and accurate description of what took place at this time in my life.

Conversations from random people started focusing on powerful personal change. I got calls from people out of the blue asking questions that frightened me and caused me to think deeply about what else might be possible.

By themselves, none of these were remarkable. In combination, and one right after the other they were leading to something and I could feel it.

One of the most peculiar was a phone call I got one night.

I had two cell phones. One that I used for work and personal life. The second cell phone was only used for one purpose, and no one had that phone number except the dealer.

That second cell phone rang. The dealer never called me and so I had never heard that phone ring. At first, I didn't even recognize the ring because I don't think I knew what it sounded like.

I was shocked. Then I was sure it had to be some kind of a wrong number. I used it only for outgoing calls, anyway. Carefully, and with some trepidation I answered the phone.

I did not recognize the voice on the other end of the phone. But the question simply blew my mind. The question was this: 'Is this the Mormon missionaries?' I did not answer, but hung up in wild surprise. The phone did not ring again.

Obviously, it could have been a legitimate wrong number. But I was so freaked out that I checked the actual number of the local Mormon missionaries. And it wasn't even close.

No amount of missed dialing or pocket dialing could've explained the difference between my phone number and the number for the missionaries.

Earlier in the book I described a "lightning bolt" type of intervention that happened my first year in college. I called it my 'first epiphany.' It left me knowing that 'I Am In Control.'

Obviously, that knowledge alone was not enough, given my fundamentally flawed foundation. I did not know it then, but part two was about to come.

# Chapter 60

# BLOOD ON THE FLOOR

A couple of nights later, on a Friday night in August, it happened. It started as a typical Friday night. I had had a couple drinks at the airport before the flight home from work and was prepared for another empty weekend. I also went to visit my son in the hospital.

After visiting my son, I settled in for the night. I was not a television watcher. In fact, it was not unusual for weeks to go by without the television ever being turned on. The kids and their friends watched TV or movies sometimes, but I simply didn't use that form of entertainment.

In a further demonstration of absurdity and excess, I had purchased the latest and largest plasma TV I could find. There it sat, with the most advanced cable service and recording technology connected, mute and dark nearly all of the time.

For some reason on this night, I turned on the television. I did not know how to use the remote or find any channels. I did not know where to find the index to see what was even on television. I messed around for a few minutes just to discover what came up.

To my surprise, I found a television program. It was called 'Intervention.' Not surprisingly, I had never heard of the program and I had no idea what it was. I knew from the set up and the discussion at the beginning that this was a depiction of a real life circumstance.

I didn't yet know what 'Reality TV' was because I didn't watch any television of any kind. So this was my first introduction to that genre of programming.

Those of you familiar with it will already see the irony. It was on the hour so the program was just starting. For some reason I felt like I should watch for a few minutes.

It quickly became evident that the program was depicting my life. The principal character was an executive with a well-paying job and an expensive substance abuse habit. The age and the substance matched my own.

I watched for 10 minutes in horror as his life fell apart.

My reaction was one of anger.

How dare anyone present to me information that showed me how messed up my life was or worst of all showed me that there were a group of people that cared about this person.

After about 15 minutes of the program, I turned off the TV and left the room. I went and did some dishes in the kitchen for about 20 minutes and came back into the living room.

It was between 40 and 45 minutes past the hour. I assumed that the program might be 30 minutes long and that it would be over by this time.

I turned the television back on, and I couldn't understand what I was seeing. At an unplanned time, in the middle of another program block, the same show began again.

I was seeing the introduction, the beginning, and the same episode playing again. This simply could not be happening. I then began to feel scared.

I did not have a hard disk recorder. How could it possibly be that some programming had been moved or interrupted to replay that program in the middle of an hour?

It became obvious to me that something else was at work here. I sat down with a slightly different feeling now and watched the program. It was exactly what I thought it was.

It was me. Presented in all of my ugliness and glory, in fairly exacting detail. Certainly there were a few differences but the similarities were overwhelming.

When it ended I got up and did a few other housekeeping things before going to bed. I couldn't stop thinking about what I had just seen. It was probably about midnight when I went to bed. The next 17 hours completely changed my life.

I woke up at 5 o'clock Saturday afternoon.

I call the time in between 'The Missing 17 Hours.'

## Chapter 61

# IT IS TIME

―――――――――――――――――――

I do not know what happened. I do not know where I was. I can only describe what took place as I experienced it.

It felt like I was out of my body. My consciousness was aware of my surroundings although I did not seem to be in the bedroom.

I seemed to be in the presence of others but I did not know who they were. I could hear voices and I felt that they were talking about me and my situation.

I was in excruciating and intense pain. The pain was both physical, spiritual and emotional. I felt as if I was being punished for the path that my life had taken.

I felt that somehow retribution of some kind was being extracted from my body and my spirit. Or, like something was being burned out of me from the inside out.

If I had to describe it in religious terms, it felt like 'hell' would feel like to someone who had to go there. Obviously I can't say, because I don't really know what happened. I only know that this experience continued for what seemed like an eternity. It went on until it ended.

I had no concept of time and no way to measure how long anything lasted. The intensity of the experience is beyond my ability to describe and so I simply say that I spent that time in intense suffering beyond that which I could conceive.

At the end of this indeterminate period, I heard a voice. Unlike the other voices which were indistinct and muffled, I could understand easily what this voice was saying.

The speech was very clear, measured and understandable. It simply said "it is enough."

The pain ended, and again after a brief time I woke up. I was in my bed almost exactly where I had laid down. It was bright daylight outside and I could tell by the light in the window that it was late in the afternoon.

I was completely confused because I didn't think I had been in bed that long. Then I noticed that all of the bedsheets, duvet and everything else were soaking wet. Completely soaked to the point that they could be wrung out.

I do not believe a body can contain that much moisture, so the idea of sweat does not make sense to me. It had no odor so I have no idea what the liquid was.

Other than the appearance of the sun, I had no concept of how much time had passed.

I felt both weak and "okay" at the same time. I got up and looked at the time and it was 5 PM Saturday afternoon. I had been somewhere for the previous 17 hours.

Again I state very clearly, I do not know what happened. I only know that I had one singular thought as I pondered on what had happened.

Everything about the process of the last several days felt divine. I knew that for some reason divine intervention had occurred again.

Despite my wish to die and the feeling that I had no value to anyone, it became clear to me that God had other ideas. He clearly had a purpose for my existence and was not about to let me die.

I determined at that moment that if God wanted me alive that badly and was willing to keep me here, with such miraculous demonstrations, then there must be something I needed to do.

I was going to find it and do it, come hell or high water.

The overwhelming realization that came to me from this experience was simple. Despite my depression, despite my own certainty that I was valueless, despite my enormous failings and despite the terrifying indictments that I ceaselessly heaped upon my head, I knew now that my judgment was flawed.

I came away with a distinct and powerful impression that constituted the second epiphany of my journey.

Simply stated — "I AM ENOUGH."

## PART III

# THE 3ᴿᴰ EPIPHANY AND WHAT TO DO NOW?

In the movies, when the great and powerful awakening occurs, the sudden epiphany, the capture of the magic amulet, then the war is over, the bad guys are defeated, the ocean goes back down, you know everything is going to be okay, the hero and the heroine smile and embrace and then they roll the credits.

We leave the theater smiling and feeling the warm pull of success and we expect ourselves somehow to reflect the power, opportunity and changes that occurred as we watched the Hero's Journey on the screen.

Real life is nothing like that. Here in the real world we have to clean up the mess and create the future. That's where this section starts.

I don't pretend to know the intricacies of divine wisdom or understand the details of the divine plan. But what I know for sure is that an intervention is not a solution.

The intervention simply stops what's going on now and make sure I understand that something else has to happen.

It provides me with some kernel of powerful wisdom but I still have to figure out the details and make things happen. At least that's how this one was and the one I received in college.

What I knew for sure is that there was a divine presence, God, who is interested in the outcome of the situation. You know from reading the book that I've been in and out of the Mormon Church.

What I knew now is that the Savior of the world, Jesus Christ, actually had more to do with us individually then I ever truly understood.

This section will take you on a journey from this epiphany up to the present day.

The battle isn't over yet, even today. Depression still strikes without warning and sometimes without mercy.

But at least by walking through this last section with me you will understand what I've done to move from death's doorway to a life of relative stability, true love, a huge desire to serve others and supreme happiness.

You will get the details of how I have integrated therapy, medicine, the love of the Savior and the treasure of a precious woman into a healthy tapestry of beauty and power.

I guess I couldn't want any more than that.

# Chapter 62

# THE RAIN

I felt a little bit like a person waking from a long nap and seeing a beautiful landscape for the first time. My mind was racing and parts of my life began to come into focus. I began for the first time in years, perhaps decades to see that maybe there was another way.

As amazing and divinely appointed as the events thus far had been, God was not finished yet. The miracles were yet to unfold over the next several weeks.

This was clearly a turning point and there could be no doubt in my mind that a new pathway lay ahead. I was yet to discover the details around the corner.

I decided to get dressed and go out to 'breakfast.' Even though it was nearly dinner time, breakfast for dinner has always been one of my favorite things. And the first meal of the day is breakfast.

I decided to go to Denny's because they serve breakfast all day. And they serve biscuits and gravy. Their sausage gravy is one of my favorite breakfast foods. I got dressed grabbed the kids that were in the house and their friends and off we went to Denny's.

I talked earlier a couple of times about the farm in Wyoming that I visited in the summer time in my grade school and junior high years. In my childhood it was a place of peace and escape.

A place where the brutality stopped and I did not feel the fear. Supervision was lighter and my mom was restrained because of the more public nature of the setting. It was also a place of many special memories.

One of these memories was the weather. In Star Valley the weather was way different then where we lived in California. Storms could come and go in a couple of hours, there was a lot more lightning.

I suppose that was because of the mountains and other features of the landscape. One of my favorite things about that little beautiful Valley was the rain. So rain is rain, right? Well, in Star Valley the rain was special.

Like anywhere else, it rained soft like a whisper sometimes and like a raging torrent at others. The clouds could be dark and fierce or light and translucent. And the rainbows were spectacular and sometimes so close you could almost touch them.

But there was one particular feature of the rain that I had only seen in Star Valley on my uncle's farm. For me, it was the symbol of the peace and calm that I felt when I was there. You might say that the same kind of rain happens in other places, but I'm sure it doesn't. Only there in that sacred Valley.

That kind of rain was precious to me. It came very slowly and languidly. The air was still and most often there was blue sky and clouds at the same time. The raindrops were very large. ALMOST as large as plums or small apricots coming down from the sky.

Now big raindrops like that should hit with the smack. Maybe they should break windows or hurt your head. But rather than hitting hard, they would land gently, almost as if they had been filled with air. And they plopped softly on the windshield or on your head or on the ground.

When the ground was dry and dusty, these gigantic drops would hit the ground and burst outwards, leaving the dust on the ground where they had landed actually dry with the water scattering out around the perimeter of the size of the raindrop.

As a child and as a growing teenager, these raindrops were very special to me and always signified peace and the gentleness of nature.

As we drove to the restaurant, I noticed it was a sunny day with beautiful weather. It was mid-August and perfect. There was a light breeze and a few puffy white clouds in the sky as we made our way through the light weekend traffic.

As you would expect, my mind was totally wrapped up in what had just happened. 'What did I need to do differently?' 'When should I start?' 'What should I do first?'

I also had begun to feel an intense overwhelming guilt because again, the realization of how much time and how many opportunities I had wasted washed over me. There I was stuck in the battle between opportunity and guilt.

About two thirds of the way to the restaurant, it happened. Star Valley rain. It began suddenly, with those great big soft drops plopping gently on the windshield.

I couldn't believe what I was seeing. It couldn't be. I had never seen that kind of rain outside of Star Valley, and besides, there weren't enough clouds in the sky to rain.

I looked up and sure enough, in the few minutes we had been driving a few clouds had gathered just overhead, and were raining that glorious, peaceful, unbelievable rain.

My eyes filled with tears, and the great big salty drops rolled down my cheeks and landed in my lap.

It would have meant nothing to anyone else. But to me, it was another evidence of not only God's desire to keep me alive, but an assurance that it was not too late, and that there was a future ahead.

## Chapter 63

# 'COLD TURKEY' AND OTHER COLD DISHES

T he day passed. The weekend passed. The next Monday came around like it always does, and the realities of life took over. Nothing on the outside was any different. Okay, I've seen a miracle. Now what?

Anyone in this sort of situation knows intuitively that the real struggle lies ahead. A lengthy addiction to alcohol, cocaine and other substances is not simply to be shrugged off in a moment.

And worst of all, what I still didn't know was that the center stage villain in the whole drama was the debilitating depression I felt, brought on by the constant chorus of 'not good enough.'

But what I knew for sure is that the drugs had to stop. There had been too many brushes with death, too many miraculous interventions and now of final 'out-of-body' experience that defied all description.

That was all well and good, but I was still terrified out of my mind. I still had no one to talk to and did not know for sure what to do next. But now I knew I wasn't alone.

Now, I had help. I had a firm and absolute knowledge that something wonderful had happened. I knew for sure that I had a purpose, that God had not abandoned me and of course I had my two epiphanies. 1) I am in control. 2) I am enough.

So I tackled the obvious. I flushed away a few thousand dollars' worth of drugs and swore I would never touch them again. I dug in mentally for the 'cold turkey' battle and waited to see what happened.

Sometimes it was terrifyingly difficult and sometimes it was almost easy to stay away from my drug of choice. I didn't know if I could do everything at once so I decided to do it in stages.

Some people think it is stupid to try to do things in stages, but it was what I did at the time. I gave up all other drugs except alcohol and I determined to drastically ration the alcohol so I would not simply substitute one for the other.

I had a cocaine relapse for one day two weeks after my Declaration of Independence. Other than that one day of relapse I have been drug-free for nearly 8 years.

I gave up alcohol seven months later and remained completely dry for over five years. The details of that period will come in a few chapters. Like I said, depression can be ruthless and relentless.

But for now, I was off to an awesome start and headed for blue skies ahead.

# Chapter 64

# TRUE COLORS

B ut let's get back to that late summer time. I had been separated for two years at that point and divorce was certain. I found it odd though that my estranged wife had taken no action before that time with regard to divorce. Perhaps she enjoyed exercising control over me through the kids.

Whatever the reason was, there was nothing in that two years of separation but acrimony and negativity that she directed towards me.

So for whatever reason, about the time that I changed and dropped all substance abuse for good, things got worse with my soon-to-be ex and her 'true colors' started to show up.

I don't know if it's always true, but it sure seems to happen a lot. People's behavior seems to change when divorce is on the near-term horizon. Maybe before it becomes an awful reality, people harbor the idea that somehow the rifts will be healed.

Whatever the reason it is, when it becomes evident that there is no way back, then agreements and understandings disappear or radically changed shape.

It's certainly true that promises and understandings that I had with my soon-to-be ex-wife were all disavowed and everything became about the money.

I found it really sad because despite the fact that she was making several hundred thousand dollars a year, her sole focus was how much more she could rip out of my heart and my life and my property.

But as I look back over my own behavior over the years, even though I was drowning in depression for decades, I can't pretend my behavior was that of an Angel. So I won't be spending much time throwing stones.

It seemed to me that every possible means was used twist and spin everything that had ever happened in our rocky relationship to be both my fault and to her advantage.

I guess that's just the name of the tune.

# Chapter 65

# MY EYES WERE OPENED

A bout three weeks later another miracle happened. I "met" someone for the first time. It was a woman who had worked in one of my departments. I had been acquainted with her for several years, but I had not really known her well.

As a high-ranking executive, it was not uncommon for me to receive free tickets to sporting events or cultural events. Almost always, these came as a pair of tickets.

When I got such tickets I did one of two things. I either gave the pair of tickets to someone in my office or I attended the event myself and randomly picked someone in the office who wanted to attend the event to go with me.

As word got out that I had tickets to a classical concert featuring the amazing cellist Yo-Yo Ma, this particular woman expressed a tremendous interest in seeing this amazing performer.

I agreed, and she met me at the concert venue downtown. We attended the concert, which was truly amazing. Anyone who has seen Yo-Yo Ma perform knows the amazing depth of his talent and the wild exuberance of his performances.

There were several other people at the event that I also was acquainted with and so during the break and at the reception afterwards I made small talk with a number of executives from other companies.

As the evening wore on and the reception neared its close, I came again to be speaking with the woman who had attended the concert from my office with my extra ticket.

Somehow I felt inclined to talk more with this woman who I did not know well. We made small talk and commented on the concert and then on office politics and recent work assignments.

In one of those 'twists of fate,' or as a matter of divine design, I became very conscious before the evening was over that this was the woman I should marry.

I know that sounds crazy. I know that everyone reading this will say that its nuts. But it was not nuts. It was divinely orchestrated and appointed.

I guess it doesn't matter what anyone thinks about it now. What matters is how I felt and what I did. And the one bedrock truth is that I was absolutely certain that it was right. It felt exactly like 'just one more' of these things that had been happening to me.

I was blown away that such a thing could even happen. I was not used to feeling anything. I was used to simply pretending my feelings in every situation. But this was a feeling I simply could not ignore. It was strong and clear and certain.

Of course I was worried that she would be completely put off by my life history and circumstance. I mean, no one in their right mind would want to get into a relationship with someone who had the miserable history of relationships that I had. No one would want to enter a relationship with a man who had a history of substance abuse and was struggling as much as I was.

And I didn't even know about suffering decades of depression yet. I only knew that I had been on this wild roller coaster for decades of suffering emotional pain, knowing for sure that I was 'not good enough' and that the consequences of all this had been terrifying.

I knew I had stumbled through multiple relationships, multiple personal disasters and suicide watch 'Armageddon' experiences. The only positive thing right now was that this recent divine intervention had helped me swear off my drug of choice.

But the feelings wouldn't go away. I decided it was now or never. I gave her a summary of those things and held my breath. She didn't seem frightened. I was flabbergasted.

Later in the evening I told her that I knew that I would marry her. I expected she would be running for the door. It didn't happen.

Pretty weird for the first introduction to someone. It wasn't even a "first date." It was simply an event we both had attended. Go figure. But God moves in mysterious ways and it's not mine to question.

I can only be profoundly grateful.

Her name is Joy.

## Chapter 66

# CHANGES COME THICK AND FAST

When I took the contract job in Alberta several years earlier I had known that it would not be a permanent assignment. The initial contract was three years.

I was not even sure that I would last long enough to complete that first three year term. The kind of work that I did had inherent opposition and was always subject to political whims.

I knew that either because of changes I made in the law or the market design or because of political changes in the government, the day would come that my contract no longer made sense for the minister or the Department of Energy.

In fact, somewhere near the beginning of my first contract I had told the minister "there will come a day when I am inconvenient." "When that day comes, I will resign." That had been our understanding from the beginning.

Surprisingly, I had finished the first three year contract and was a bit more than a year into a new three-year contract when the Yo-Yo Ma concert took place.

Well, just a few days after that amazing night, the predicted day came. Political changes had recently taken place in the government at the highest levels.

The new premier had come under intense lobbying from some market participants and was completely unprepared for the intensity of the ambush.

I was made aware that my presence was creating a problem for the minister and the premier at this point and that it would be best if I resigned.

The next day I terminated the contract.

I got the severance I had negotiated and began to think about what to do next. Several contract and job opportunities came up right away. Some locally where I lived and some back in the states.

However, somewhere deep in my heart I knew that if I took another job doing the same things, the likely outcome would be more of the same. I would be doomed to repeat the same cycles as in the past.

That, above all things, was not going to happen.

# Chapter 67

# SO THIS IS LOVE

n the same few days between the concert and my resignation that the political realities developed, the relationship between Joy and I had developed at an astounding speed.

Not only was she unfazed by my declarations of intent to marry her, she had not objected to the idea that this was a desirable outcome. I wasn't sure what this all meant, but I was moving forward in my mind anyway.

I had not actually proposed at this point, but the intention was clear and definitely in the air.

Five minutes after the meeting where I agreed to resign I walked into Joy's office and closed the door.

I said 'well, you may want to cancel this whole thing.' I knew she was not expecting that I would suddenly be unemployed or be moving to some distant location.

I explained what had happened and that starting the next day, I would be resigning my position to facilitate my promise to the minister and his deputy.

I said again 'you will want to thoroughly reconsider what we've been talking about.' 'I know this is not what you planned, and if you want to scrap this whole thing, I will understand.'

She didn't hesitate for one minute. I was completely blown away.

Nothing frightened her. She was an absolute bulletproof rock. She went all in from the first moment and has never wavered since. The certainty that this was divine intervention that came the first moment of our meeting has never changed.

I had never met anyone like this or seen such a demonstration of loyalty and certainty in my whole life.

Everything about love and affection and acceptance in my entire life had been conditional.

Love in my family growing up was conditioned on behavior and obedience. If you were 'bad,' you were out. If you didn't follow the rules, you were worthless.

Nothing in any of my prior marriages or relationships even approached this new feeling I was experiencing for the first time.

Being introduced to something so completely unconditional was totally outside of anything I had known. I simply did not know what to make of it.

I was overwhelmed. At the same time I felt completely unworthy of such devotion I felt both expansive and shriveled up at the same time.

I know that makes no sense at all. But nothing about depression and its contradictory feelings and irrational juxtapositions makes any sense.

She resigned her position two weeks later. This was not a move of stupidity or desperation.

This was an intelligent, capable, educated, successful and self-sufficient woman who had made quite a life for herself for decades.

She had owned several businesses. She regularly took trips on her own to Europe. She was quite capable of managing her life without anyone's help yet she had chosen to throw her lot in completely with me.

I was speechless with amazement and as I write this now years later I am still overcome with emotion at the immediacy, certainty and power of her commitment.

We took a trip to Italy and did some tremendously fun things to celebrate our new relationship.

Three and one-half months after that spectacular concert we got married in an intimate and private wedding. Some of my children and their friends attended our beautiful ceremony.

We took a fun winter honeymoon trip and began our life adventure with the most spectacular and sincere of expectations.

And as it always does, the honeymoon has to end sometime. After all of the fun happens, you still have to get down to business and create a real life made out of substance, not wishes.

# Chapter 68

# ENTREPRENEURSHIP

W e carefully considered the jobs that I was offered. Some were local and allowed us to stay in Alberta. Some would require a move to the US.

We thought about what moving would mean, we thought about what staying would mean since we had opportunities to do both.

In the end we cast a vote for sanity. We decided that staying in the same career would likely result in some of the same problems that had happened before.

I turned down all the jobs.

We had both owned businesses before and so being self-employed wasn't new. Joy had owned several antique stalls and was a long time eBay marketer.

I had owned a recording studio where I had recorded songs for Grammy-winning artists. I had also been a performing artist and had several albums to my credit.

Joy had been operating to antique stalls and her eBay business part time as a hobby. Since she was quite expert in these areas our first move was simply to expand the size of that business right away.

The only business I wanted to be in was the music business. But I had stopped doing that professionally some 15 years earlier. So I would need to get completely refreshed on current studio techniques, production processes and other changes in the recording arts and sciences.

Success as a recording artist also assumed that I would immediately be able to start writing songs again and creating music that would sell.

This is where depression raises its ugly head. Fear began to take over and I started worrying that the things I would write wouldn't be successful.

There was no real reason for this fear. The music I had produced before had received a lot of radio time and had sold successfully on the open market. So I knew, intellectually, that this was possible.

Knowing something is possible intellectually and having the courage to make it happen when you struggle with depression are two different things.

But at this point in the story, I had never been diagnosed and did not know after all these decades that that was the root of the terrible fear and malaise that would overcome me.

The one time that I had considered being treated for depression years before had slipped into the background since I had successfully overcome my massive cocaine use.

So we blasted forward. Joy was running two antique stalls and an eBay business and I outfitted a studio and began recording music.

Alcohol was still part of my life, but I was successfully moderating its use for the most part. There were some incidents of excessive drinking, but in the excitement of the new relationship and our newly chosen business direction, they faded into the background.

Still, in those first few months, alcohol use was a problem often enough to worry both of us. I knew that my journey to sanity was still a work in progress.

What I didn't know was that even though giving up alcohol was critical, it was not the main attraction. Something else far more sinister was still lurking in the shadows.

## Chapter 69

# BACK TO GOD

E ven though much of my life felt like it was on a path to improvement, I knew that there were parts that were still damaged and were in need of repair.

I started feeling like I should explore returning to faith. Even though much of my earlier experience with religion had been warped by my mom's fanatic interpretations and her brutality, I knew that in order to have peace of mind I had to get myself right with God.

I started talking to Joy about churches and religion in general. I didn't really know what her religious experience had been or how she felt about any of that, because we hadn't discussed it much in our relationship so far.

That might seem strange since religion is often a point of contention in relationships, but I had been so certain in my knowledge that I was doing the right thing that I knew that there would be a way to work this out.

In our discussions, Joy told me that she had been raised mostly without much religious observance. Her parents were Ukrainian Orthodox by tradition, but they had not been practicing members except at the occasional feast day or family celebration.

Most recently, she had studied Buddhism. This had been mostly driven by a need she felt during her father's terminal battle with cancer three years earlier.

The only religious tradition I had known was that of Mormon. Deep down, I knew that the doctrine of that church was true. But I also knew that something about my own experience did not square with those things that I knew must be true about God.

Somehow I had to find the way to bridge the gap between my previous experience with that church which had been dominated by punishment, guilt and negativity and the fact that the Savior I knew taught repentance, forgiveness and peace of conscience.

The bottom line was that if I was returning to God, it had to be real and not in any way based on previous experience or circumstance.

I was grateful that Joy felt inclined to participate. Her first experience in attending a Mormon meeting with me was wonderful for her. She reported feeling immediately at home the minute she entered the building and the chapel. She didn't share this feeling with me until several days later.

In the years that have followed, she has often referred to the feeling of immediate comfort and love that she experienced immediately on entering the chapel. It turned out to be a profound indicator for her that she was on the right path.

We discussed the idea of her taking missionary discussions to learn about the doctrine of the church. She decided she wanted to do that. After a few weeks, Mormon missionaries came over regularly and taught Joy the basic principles and tenants of the church.

It was powerful for me to participate in this process with her. I mostly just watched and talked to her about her feelings after the missionaries left. My own feeling for God was being rekindled and Joy was becoming receptive to the church doctrine, the people and the teachings.

During this time I was also able to completely give up alcohol. This completed my freedom from the drugs I had used to mask my feelings of worthlessness.

About seven months after our initial meeting, or two months after we got married, I gave up drinking for good. Or so I thought at the time.

Joy was baptized about a month after I quit drinking.

On the one hand I was excited about her joining the church and sharing that journey with me. On the other hand I had not yet come to understand my own depression and the cyclical nature of that affliction.

Depression comes and goes. With me it had come hard and fast many times but also receded when things seem to be going well. Things were moving smoothly and well at this point and I was grateful and happy in our direction. But future battles had yet to be won.

As I reflect on this now and write this narrative, I am still totally overwhelmed at the graciousness of God in providing for me a companion that was so perfect for me and so spectacular at the same time. I had never been in a relationship that was a true partnership.

In fact, I didn't know what a partnership looked like. Because I was so 'broken' myself I had never been in a position to help in previous relationships.

Each of those relationships had been started with a person who suffered deeply in her own way from her own childhood experience. Each was founded in a situation fraught with difficulty that I was completely unaware of.

I realize that everyone has their own struggles. That's just how life is.

But each of the women I had chosen had extremely troubled backgrounds and deep issues of their own they had not been aware of or dealt with. My lack of knowledge about the symptoms they were exhibiting and help I might be able to offer was a barrier to getting help we could have used.

The fact that I was suffering from undiagnosed and untreated serious depression made me incapable and essentially unavailable for appropriate support in those relationships.

The depression wasn't the only thing. The very recent epiphany that "I Am Enough," was still sinking in, and I really wasn't sure how to turn that into an actionable plan yet.

I still had an unhealthy need to seek approval from people who had abused me. Even in my mid-50s, I had an unhealthy and debilitating obsession to get a virtual 'stamp of approval' on my forehead that finally and definitively said 'you're okay.'

This really meant that the monster that created and drove my depression, the underlying feeling that I was 'fundamentally flawed' and would 'never be good enough,' still stood in stark contrast to the new feeling of 'I AM ENOUGH.'

In this situation however God had prepared a woman of enormous strength and patience. She demonstrated a willingness to be independent and strong and walk me down this path of healing. I will forever be grateful for this divinely appointed circumstance in my life.

The path we had yet to walk was fierce, dark, terrifying and full of struggles. Even with the two great epiphanies that had been given to me and the great gift that Joy represented, the monster of depression would not go down easily.

# Chapter 70

# TAKING JOY HOME TO MOM

―――――――――――――――――――

A s I look back now, it's easy to see that I was still in a precarious situation. I had been helped a great deal by "divine intervention." I have been given the unbelievable gift of a companion who was finally healthy for a change instead of being one of two broken people in a relationship.

But the driver in my actions was still to seek approval in an unhealthy way from those past characters in my life drama. Particularly my mom. So immediately, I took my new wife Joy to my mom's house for 'approval.'

Of course I didn't think about it that way, but looking at it now it feels like I was saying: 'See, I have a beautiful new girl who loves me, and all of your fear that I will die under a bridge and go to hell is groundless. Can I please be okay now?'

Surprisingly, my mom showed verbal approval. Except she was extremely nervous because I didn't 'have a job.' In her world, the idea of being an entrepreneur did not give her comfort.

That is strange given the fact that she was raised on a farm, lived in the old Homestead and her brother lived next door and was still successfully running the farm.

Everyone had a job, right? She was certain that I was going to fail and not do my duty in providing for my family. Everything was framed in terms of duty and 'right and wrong.'

I really don't know what she was actually thinking. Only one third of all of this was spoken. The rest was a dialogue in my own mind based on past experience.

The real irony is that I don't even need to care what she thinks. I get to create my own life and be my own person. That is my divine right, your divine right and cannot be taken from us.

Foolishly, I was still giving mine away. But at that juncture, I was still depressed, undiagnosed and untreated and had not cut the apron strings. I didn't know I had 'grown up' yet.

I was starting on the long, precarious, endless journey of regaining the approval status of my family. It sounds pretty sick for me to say that now in this book, but that is actually what was going on.

The same family that had prevented me from participating in family events when they didn't approve of me, the same family that had blamed my sin and unworthiness for every struggle that had come into my life and the same family that had taken the opposite side in every dispute.

Not much of a place of support, particularly for someone going through the depression struggles that I had fought with and was still fighting with.

I admit, it's pretty crazy trying to get the approval of people you know deep inside of you will never give you the approval you seek. You will never be 'good enough' for them. You will never be 'okay' in their judgment.

Things that you have done and the things that have happened in your life have already tainted you beyond repair.

The powerful truth is really that they don't get to judge. They don't get to decide if you are enough. Their opinion matters exactly ZERO in the final analysis. You are your own judge. God is the only arbiter. And the rest of these opinions amount to nothing.

But I didn't know that yet. I know that now.

So in the fog of depression, I was struggling for approval yet again, and with great gusto and renewed desperation I launched into that impossible project.

## Chapter 71

# TEN YEARS TO NEVER

———————————————

When you get excommunicated from the Mormon Church it's both a punishment and an opportunity. The punishment comes because you lose your 'sacraments' and your standing in the church.

There is also some stigma associated with it and some members treat you poorly although the church preaches vigorously against this bias and discrimination.

The opportunity is one of repentance. By being outside the church, you have the opportunity of following a path of repentance, working with your local priesthood leaders and making a choice about whether or not you want to return to full fellowship.

You are allowed to attend all church meetings while you are excommunicated and often many members of the congregation don't even know your status. But you are not allowed to participate, take the sacrament or hold any positions in the congregation.

If it's something you want to do, and the choice is always fully in your control you can choose the path of readmission into the church. After a period of time of obedience and diligence you can ask to be readmitted into the church through baptism.

This baptism is important, because it signifies a cleansing from sin. You are then forgiven of past sin as far as the church is concerned, and can approach your own life and relationship to God as if things were new.

It's important to note that the doctrine of the church also specifies that this is all contingent on complete honesty. If you are lying or hiding sins of any nature, then all of this is a sham and you are just one more lying hypocrite.

I wanted to come back into the church for two reasons. Subconsciously knowing that I would never get approval from my family, I at least wanted to have the approval of the church whose doctrine I still believed.

At least if the church and its leaders felt I had sufficiently changed to allow me back into the church through baptism and thus outwardly mark a new era in my life, I could take comfort in that and perhaps relegate the pain of familial disapproval to a lower volume.

The second reason was that I still believed in the doctrine of the church. The realization that my mom had been abusive and was outside of the doctrine and the law in her behavior was slowly crystallizing in my mind.

Joy was marvelously helpful in helping me see what a healthy childhood could have been and how badly outside the boundaries my own experience was.

She also spent hundreds of hours helping me see how the choices and circumstances of my life tied so closely to my feeling of 'not being good enough,' and how I had abdicated my own freedom of choice to the opinions of others.

All this meant is that I held no resentment at having been excommunicated from the church. The behavior I had exhibited in ending my previous marriage was certainly not in harmony with their teachings and certainly not a demonstration of any behavior consistent with the doctrine.

Having given up drugs, alcohol and every other habit that was keeping me hostage, and with Joy having embraced the faith by her recent baptism, I decided to make a run at returning to the church. As I mentioned, that requires that you get permission from the local presiding authorities.

I spoke with my bishop who is the presiding authority in the local geographic area where you live. He was encouraging and told me I needed to speak with the stake president.

The stake president is a lay leader who presides over a larger jurisdiction of ten or so geographically defined wards. Sucking it up inside I made an appointment.

I described my situation to the stake president and indicated the desire that I had to return to the church. I then asked him what I needed to do to get started on the path.

He outlined the procedure. There were two parts to the process. The first part is a period of time where you demonstrate obedience and willingness to live the doctrines of the church. After that time you are readmitted into the church by baptism.

He told me that this first step might be achievable in as little as two or three years.

The second part is a 'restoration of blessings.' This means that the sacraments and ordinances that you had received, but that were nullified by your excommunication, are reinstated.

This is critical because it constitutes a true symbol from the church that you are returned to your status and standing and they treat you as if the failures had not happened.

He then told me that in his opinion the second part would not happen for '10 years to never.' I left the interview that day wanting to give up and die.

I felt like the church was the right place to be. The teachings were right. I had a 'testimony,' or a personal witness of its truthfulness.

I was sad. I was hurt. I was afraid that it really meant that even God thought I was 'not good enough.' But I wasn't ready to give up.

There wasn't anything I could do about it so Joy and I simply continued going to church on a regular basis. I assumed that after some time I would ask again and see how things stood.

The opinion he expressed did not change my belief in God or Jesus or any of the doctrines, but it was very discouraging with respect to the future with the church.

I was also afraid.

Chapter 72

# BACK TO THE FAMILY?

You can see by now that all I was doing was repeating the behaviors at the beginning of my second marriage. This time however, I was married to a sane woman who would not let me make trades like I had when I alienated my two older children to satisfy my second wife and my mom.

Joy stood her ground and helped me stand mine. She asked me repeatedly if I really thought I needed the approval of anyone in my family. She must have asked me this question a million times.

I could dimly see her points but somehow still believed that she just didn't understand. Of course the reality is that it was me that didn't see clearly.

So somehow trying to walk a line between Joy's wisdom and my faulty need for approval, I began clawing my way back up the social ladder of my family.

After we were married two years, I was invited to my first family reunion in over a decade. Joy was cautious and not sure she wanted to go. She came to protect me as much as to meet people.

When I was at the family reunion, I came to understand that contact between my mom, my siblings and all my nieces and nephews had been fairly regular and frequent.

I gradually learned that the lack of contact between me and the rest of the family had been intentional. I had been deleted from the family lists and Christmas rotation and other social features because they 'didn't know how I would respond.'

In other words, I was the black sheep that was not welcome. I was the bastard at the family reunion. I was indeed 'not good enough' and might have poisoned the atmosphere or damaged their children or perpetrated some other evil.

This was full-blown proof of the total breakdown of closeness and support that I could have experienced from a healthy family. That just means our family was dysfunctional.

I I now realize that it's all they know how to do, they are all struggling in their own way. It would be foolish from me to expect anything else. But I remain hopeful. If I can change, so can they.

I'm not sure what the impetus for change in these relationships would be or what needs to happen to get it started, but I always believe that a brighter future can be created by those who choose it.

However, at that time, my warped sense of obligation to receive approval kept kicking in. Emotionally I felt that I would never be 'all the way put back together' until I got my mom's approval. And was back on the family Christmas card list.

Now I realize that it may never happen. Everyone reacts differently to circumstances in their lives. Everyone has to walk their own path of development. Everyone has to do what they feel is best for their own lives.

My failings, multiple divorces, major depression, going through rehab, drug addiction, being in and out of the church and other drama was just another circumstance that they saw in a family member's life.

They may be too frightened or uninformed or uninterested to reach out and be part of my healing journey. Maybe they just don't want to. Maybe they're struggling with their own deep demons.

That's actually okay and each of them must walk whatever path they choose for their own development and happiness. Now that I'm finally beginning to get healthy, I have the opportunity to reach out and see what I might be able to do for them.

## Chapter 73

# WHO TEACHES CHILDREN TO HATE?

M eanwhile, my third ex-wife had custody of the three youngest girls. She pretty much hated my guts and wanted me to die. Remember, she kept telling me how badly she wanted to wake up in a world where I did not exist.

She actively did, and still does everything in her power to alienate and destroy the relationship and feeling that these three girls might have with me. I know this goes on even today, because I still get reports through the grapevine.

I know that sounds harsh and judgmental. It is. It is also the truth. I'm not going to spend precious words or minutes of your time describing the incidents to try to prove anything to you.

It would be a waste of time, so I will just state it and leave it for you to make up your own mind. My attorney even remarked that in all his decades of practice he had never seen such a vindictive, deceitful woman.

The purpose of this chapter is to describe my feeling of helplessness and explore a very real and ongoing consequence of my illness. During my time of deep depression, I was not available to them emotionally and failed them as a dad.

She used this at the time to create hatred and alienation between them and me.

Now that I am in a far healthier circumstance, I struggle not only against overcoming past mistakes and their very real consequences but also against her

181

active campaigning to perpetuate further alienation and negativity because she hates me for leaving the relationship.

She spared no effort. After I got clean from drugs and started returning to church she realized there was no more leverage she could have from my bad behavior.

So she went after Joy and her character. She attacked Joy even though she did not even have the privilege of an acquaintance. Typical jealous and vindictive ex-spouse behavior on steroids. The family therapist we were seeing at the time told me some of the epithets that my ex-wife had used.

Regardless of the reason, the sad outcome was that she was successful in destroying the relationship between the three youngest girls and me.

Two short incidents will be enough to illustrate the point. One involved the martial arts swords I talked about several chapters ago. As you recall, these swords were not sharpened and were for display purposes only.

They hung with their point facing downward flush against the wall coming down the staircase. The handles did not protrude from the wall more than the distance of an ordinary picture frame. The points of the swords were flush against the wall.

My 11-year-old daughter reported that she was in fear of her life because coming down the staircase she dropped an apple and it had impaled itself on one of the swords. This is a physical impossibility, nevertheless this dramatic imaginary incident was the basis for mortal fear.

Another far more vicious incident was a story created that Joy and I had invited the girls into our bedroom when we were not dressed. This was simply a bald lie but typical of the sort of concocted nonsense.

Another thing that I suspected was that our return to the church was also a pivotal contributor to her campaign for alienation. My ex-wife despises the Mormon Church and believes that it is a cult and the source of vile and reprehensible people.

Five months after I got married, the girls announced they didn't want to come over to the house anymore. She manipulated them into a contrived meeting at a Starbucks where the three of them sat around the table and made the pronouncement.

My ex-wife sat across the mall supervising from a distance.

That was a blow to Joy and me, but I had expected nothing less.

Though I have sent Christmas cards and birthday cards for years, these three youngest girls remain steadfast in their desire to have no contact with me at this time.

This is extremely painful. It is one more complete indication that somehow I am 'fundamentally flawed' and cannot be repaired. I struggle with this, even today as I write this book.

I choose to remain optimistic, and have done and will do everything I can to repair and rekindle these relationships which are so precious to me. I know things can change. I know the future will be different.

About three months after that 'announcement' happened I began to have the feeling that we needed to move. It was just time to start in a new place.

There was too much baggage from the old drug days and other things that had gone on in that house to be a place for good healing.

Having turned down several employment opportunities, and launching our entrepreneurial endeavors we were free to go where we thought would be best.

We took an exploratory drive through Oregon, California, Nevada, Arizona, Utah, Wyoming and Montana. We both had the strong feeling that moving to the US was a good choice.

Chapter 74

# THERE *IS* A GOD

O ften throughout this book I have referred to divine intervention, divine
help and other manifestations of my belief in a God and a purpose
for life.

To be clear, I am a strong believer in God, Jesus Christ and the Christian
tradition. I have faith that God is a loving, kind being who has nothing but our
best interests at heart. I have come to know these things for myself.

I also know that Jesus Christ performed an atoning sacrifice that in some
unfathomable way made it possible to cleanse our souls from the stains of
mistakes. That doesn't mean we don't suffer or have to fix stuff ourselves where
we can, it just means that He has created a path to healing.

I have been astounded over and over again at the patience that God has
exhibited while He has carefully molded my life and offered me a path to places
of healing and health.

Realizing that God was available but also that He was never going to force
His way into my life, I chose to begin making prayer a part of my regular practice.
I wanted all the help I could get.

On our lengthy road trip through the states, we looked at some real estate
for a couple days in Phoenix. One particular house felt immediately like the
place we needed to move. There aren't any other words to use except to say it
felt inspired.

After much thought and prayerful consideration we opted to move to the Phoenix area. The real estate prices were good. In addition, that is where I had operated my recording studio for a dozen years.

On top of that, Joy had a longtime interest in the Indians of the Southwest. The Heard Museum, the largest museum in the world covering the Southwest native tribes is located in Phoenix. Joy had been a member for several years and wanted to explore being a docent there.

Her dad had been an archaeologist and had a lot of experience working with first Nations tribes and their artifacts in the western part of Canada and the US.

One of the most important reasons to choose Phoenix was that our oldest son from my first marriage, lived in the Phoenix area with his family. This meant we could be close to him. He had several kids and I wanted to be able to be a grandpa as well.

He was the older of the two children that I essentially abandoned after getting married to my second wife and giving in to pressure from her and my mom.

The decision to not have much contact with my two oldest children in order to make my mom happy and my second wife, is one I regret with all my heart to this day.

He had a successful and celebrated career as an All-American heavyweight wrestler for Arizona State University. He had also tried out for the US Olympic team shortly after graduating from college.

I had only peripherally participated in his wrestling career. I was able to go to the Olympic tryouts. I felt ashamed at my lack of participation and wanted somehow to make up for lost time.

Back in Canada we started making plans for the move. Of the four children who have been living with us, there were two left.

The two oldest had graduated from high school and were living on their own. Both had jobs and did not want to move away from Canada. One was attending school as well.

We started planning for the move in August. The plan was for the two children still at home to come with us to Arizona.

When we left for Arizona in December, just one of the children ended up coming. The other had received a job offer that was exciting and she elected to move in with a friend and remain behind.

From the point of view of my depression, there was enough activity and progress that this was one of the times it appeared to be in 'remission.'

I don't know if that word is used with depression or other mental illnesses, but it simply felt like it was not controlling things at the time.

This was deceptive however, because at the same time as all of these changes, I was still desperately clawing for, hoping for, and working for the stamp of approval from my family.

It was just that there were no outward manifestations.

# Chapter 75

# ARIZONA

W e bought a house. We moved to Arizona. We started a new chapter.

Once in Arizona we set up business right away. Joy began her antique business on eBay in earnest. I imagined that with extreme work and dedication everything would be fine. I always think that if I just work hard enough, everything is okay.

But the fundamental issues around depression don't evaporate. They go into recession and reappear with unpredictable frequency and ruthless rage. That comes shortly.

We began having business success. Joy's eBay store did well. I created a meditation course and wrote five books on the topic. I got it up on the Internet.

We made some sales. Like any business, there were periods of excitement and periods of big discouragement. But the burning fire of 'if I could just do a little more, I'll be okay,' was still controlling every aspect of my feeling and actions.

The course on meditation sold online but was not successful enough to pay the bills so I started about thinking about something else to go with it.

We were still fighting bitter battles from my last divorce. My ex-wife lied about our agreements and refused to implement the settlement she had signed.

I had to hire an attorney. I could not access the money I had saved and what I was earning was not enough to pay all the bills.

Depression came again in the wake of my failure to be successful. Even though I knew it was not true, I started feeling like this was all some form of retribution for my terrible life.

I could not get the three youngest girls to communicate with me. I blamed myself. Other normal things took place that were disappointing. To the lens of depression, they were all giant red arrows screaming at my face that I was unworthy.

Slowly, my certainty and good feeling started to evaporate.

# Chapter 76

# THE MIRACLES

There was one amazing and powerful bright spot in this whole situation. Again, as it usually does this concerns God and his love.

The Mormon Church is mostly administered on a geographic basis. I went to the local leaders of the church here in Arizona and explained to them everything that it happened while we lived in Canada.

I also explained the "ten years to never" assessment of the leader we had spoken with in Canada. I was forthright and honest and did not leave out any details.

I gave them the names and phone numbers of the Bishop and Stake President I had worked with in Canada so they could have any conversations they thought would be appropriate.

To my grateful astonishment, the stance here was different. The processes and steps were the same, but the prognosis and the length of time was considerably different.

The responsibility for those decisions is in the hands of the local leaders, so I was simply enormously grateful that the prospect had changed from never to more near-term.

About four years later I was finished with the entire process. I was back as a member of the church in full fellowship with all of my blessings and sacraments restored.

Joy and I were married in the temple, which in the Mormon tradition is an important and powerful blessing. God had been gracious to us once again.

Though my spiritual progress was good, business progress was very slow. However, we kept moving forward with our businesses and expected with enough hard work that things would turn out well.

# Chapter 77

# CREATING A NEW BUSINESS

A fter a year of fits and starts, I abandoned the idea of teaching meditation online. I had sold some courses and knew that I could eventually build it up, but it did not really match the best use of the talents I had developed.

We decided that my most effective use of these talents would be as a business coach. I had a lot of experience owning businesses and accelerating business success for others.

I explored online opportunities to study this field of coaching and get myself quickly certified. Given my rich executive background I figured I could get a coaching certification fairly quickly.

I found a credible and accredited institution where I took courses and tests online and in person. I achieved the 'Professional Coach' designation and a 'Master Coach' designation. I was all set.

I began getting speaking opportunities at different business events and Internet marketing events around the country. As was my custom in business, success came fairly quickly. It seemed then for a time that everything would be just great.

But just like any new endeavor, there are ups and downs and it actually takes a lot of work. I don't mind the hard work and it is something I am both good at and accustomed to.

But marketing online is a funny thing. It is a different skill set and requires different tools, focus and activities than traditional marketing and business growth.

I needed to learn a whole new set of skills and think about things in a completely different way to match the digital economy. I studied and worked diligently, but working in your own business, it's easy to get lost and discouraged

The problem for me is the mental battle that takes place when the dry spells occur. Depression, sadness and a growing fear of 'not being good enough' crept in again when no one was looking.

Even at this time I had still not been diagnosed or treated in any way for depression. I simply assumed that the things I experienced were normal and that if I just 'tried harder' it would be okay.

Let's get one thing really clear. When you have depression 'trying harder' is not the answer. I did not know I was suffering from 35 years of depression.

I had not addressed the root causes of my depression. I did not have the tools to understand when it began to control my feeling, my energy, my outlook and my behavior.

I begin to experience periods of anger and of profound guilt and sadness. I became certain that my opportunities had passed and that I was doomed to failure or mediocrity the rest of my life.

# Chapter 78

# WHAT THE HELL?

B ecause I blamed myself for lack of business success, I did not discuss these growing feelings with Joy. She sensed that something was wrong and tried to help. I just assumed it was my failure and I needed to fix it.

I had not yet acquired either the good sense or the skill to discuss my feelings openly with another human being. I had spent so much of my life in isolation that openness was a new experience for me.

In my extended family, we began to be get some initial signs of approval. That meant a bit more contact, invites to family reunions and some degree of inclusion in the ebb and flow of the extended family goings-on.

But, everyone reacts differently to life's vicissitudes. Some of my brothers and sisters had been completely repulsed by my behavior and found it unpleasant to have any contact.

In fact, they created reasons not to talk to me and found it difficult to be around me. One even requested I not talk about them in the quarterly newsletter I had been creating for our 10 children.

Others, as you would expect, were more open. I began finding some level of relationship with them. It was slow. The years of isolation created awkwardness and apathy.

In addition, we were operating in the framework of 'you've got to prove yourself before you're okay.' I certainly didn't have enough years under my belt to cross that threshold.

I reflected how strange this all was. When my kids succeeded I rejoiced with them. When my kids failed I supported them. When things got tough I tried to help.

In my worldview, when someone you love is struggling, you empathize, you help, you give advice if it's useful and you do what you can to improve the situation.

Later, when something changes and the situation improves, you rejoice with them. You congratulate them. You are joyful and participate with love in the positive changes and growth that have taken place in their life.

I still don't see anything like that in my extended family. I rarely felt genuine concern or that anyone was actually interested in what was going on in my life beyond calling me out on some aberrant behavior. That may sound harsh, but that's how it felt.

Occasionally I would get the periodic letter that tried to express some empathy. Generally any empathy and interest was buried in the preaching against my evil.

The undertone was always 'you are getting what you deserve, you poor miserable outcast. Maybe someday you'll do something different and then we can stand to be around you when you won't contaminate us.'

I still didn't have sense enough to just dismiss the whole lot of them. I still craved that final approval from the one place it would never come. In my quiet moments I was still a failure.

That exacerbated the feeling that I was 'not good enough' and never would be until I met some standard of approval that was unknown, unwritten and unreachable.

Warped, I know, but that's where I lived.

So let's take stock of where we are. This is something I can do now in the book so you get a complete picture, but not something I did at that time.

I am in a happy and stable relationship with a spectacular woman.

I have a business that is growing but not fast enough.

I have several children who are unresponsive to my efforts to create a relationship.

I am still defining my ultimate value by the level of 'approval' from my mom.

I was creating a repeat of history.

I was happily married, in the church, and striving to re-obtain the approval of my mom and family. Somehow, I imagined that this time was different. But of course, it's not.

Nothing had fundamentally changed.

I was not addressing the root cause, which was recurring depression stemming from my abusive upbringing and the repeated cycles of success and self-sabotage.

I did not know what was broken.

## Chapter 79

# RESISTANCE IS FUTILE—OH *NO*, NOT AGAIN!

From the outside, things seemed smooth. We had been married and very happy for six years. But on the inside, things were different. I had not overcome the habit of living life on two levels.

In the last chapter I listed the things that were not going according to plan. Because I perceived all these deficiencies as my fault, I found myself being plagued by an increasing sense of isolation.

I was making attempts to repair relationships with the older two children and was meeting with some good success, but could not stop dwelling on what might've been.

I began to be overwhelmed with the notion that everything was my fault and that no matter what happened nothing would ever really be okay.

I had three big goals.

First, I wanted to build up a successful business based on business coaching, speaking opportunities and writing a few books. That was underway, but growing too slowly and I felt deficient in how much money I was making. 'Not fast enough' was shaking her finger at me.

Second, I wanted to climb back up the family hierarchy, and garner the approval that I had somehow never been able to get. I thought that this would be the final way to eliminate the gnawing cancer of 'not good enough' that was devouring my heart.

Third, I wanted to fix all of the relationships with all of my children. I wept regularly over how I had failed. I had a vision of what 'should have been' if I hadn't been broken. I expected myself to create that.

I think one of the motivators for this third goal was the fact that I had no closeness with my brothers and sisters. I desperately wanted my kids to have something better with their siblings. But I was failing. 'Fundamentally flawed' was clucking her tongue.

As I mentioned in the last chapter, I published a newsletter that I put out quarterly with a section for each of the kids. I wanted them to share information, activities and feelings so they would have a closeness I never had. I sent it to all of the kids, even those who were not talking to me.

I also sent the normal birthday and Christmas cards and presents.

Some of the kids rejected my efforts, but gradually over time it seemed to move from rejection to tacit acceptance. I don't know if the girls got the gifts or cards I sent. But I tried to keep it up anyway.

Over time the trio of 'not good enough,' 'not fast enough,' and 'fundamentally flawed' started singing louder than any other music going on in my life.

I was sinking again.

Chapter 80

# DOES IT EVER END?

J oy did not know anything about the battle that was going on in my heart. I
had never known how to share that with anyone, and this situation was no
exception. It certainly wasn't any failing on her part, I simply didn't know
how to be close to anyone.

This is where real friendship could come in. I had never learned how to be
a friend or how to make a friend effectively. I can say that now because at the
time of this writing, and through Joy's perseverance and love, I have begun to
understand this wonderful gift.

But at that time I was still convinced that everything in life was conditional
and that if I shared my true inner battles with anyone, they would simply validate
my feeling of inadequacy. Depression. An evil, life-sucking, debilitating monster

All of the things that I was trying to do to reestablish myself and gain approval
in 'the family' were marginally effective. Some days I thought I was winning at
creating a place in the 'family hierarchy,' and some days I thought I was losing.

In truth, it didn't matter. But I didn't know that then.

The relationships with our kids got better and worse and then better again.
Overall the progress seemed to be in the upward direction and I felt pretty
good about it. But the awful words 'what could it have been like?' wouldn't
leave me alone.

Every person goes through struggles as they grow up and find their place
in the world. That's completely normal and our kids were no exception. One of

my biggest stumbling blocks was that I consistently blamed myself for all the struggles the kids were having.

It certainly did not help that two of my ex-wives spared no effort in reinforcing the notion ever at every opportunity.

I heard regular reports through the grapevine of conversations still claiming that I was the evil one, responsible for all failings and that everything from the Holocaust to world hunger was my fault.

The stupid thing was that because of my depression I believe that.

One thing I was skilled was at self-loathing. The combination of these circumstances triggered a downward spiral. It was slow at first but progressed over time until I was locked in a feeling of hopelessness and helplessness without realizing what was going on.

My efforts at building my business became lethargic and I struggled to get things created that I wanted and needed to get created for our businesses.

Fortunately, Joy was moving the eBay business forward at full steam and we were okay financially even though I felt like I was failing us as a couple.

I began blaming myself for lack of immediate growth and was unable to decipher the connection between my emotional malaise and the slow growth of the businesses.

In the depressed mind this sort of circle becomes a lethal cyclone very quickly. Once you get hooked in it, there is no way out without a full-blown interruption and some help.

I descended deeper and deeper into a state of cloudiness and worthlessness. I began questioning the value of life and certainly the value of my contribution to anyone that I knew that was living.

Like Godzilla roaring on to the screen to devour the hero at the climax of the movie my courage completely failed. Consideration of suicide became very real. I thought ending it all might actually be the right thing to do because it would relieve everyone of my evil presence.

I had not had a drink in five years. But now, for two terrifying days I sat with a bottle in one hand and a gun in the other. I knew life was out of control.

# Chapter 81

# I'M NOT ALONE

When Joy saw how serious this had become, she rose to the challenge and basically stood for me when no one else ever had.

With her help and the help of some local church leaders I made it through the terror of 'The Name Of The Black,' without inflicting physical harm on myself.

But the emotional toll was enormous. For months, with Joy's help and with a counselor, I was digging myself out of this hole. With this counselor, I had my first real discussions about depression.

I began to see that my emotional framework was shattered. There was something else wrong here that I had never considered.

During this recovery this period, Joy and I talked a lot about what depression looked like in real life and how it might be related to much of my story.

For the first time in my life, I began to truly consider the possibility that depression was the reason I had struggled emotionally so seriously for decades.

It may be ridiculously obvious to someone else, but to me, the idea that I had a 'mental illness' was like saying I was a subhuman and despicable person.

The dogma of my childhood said 'mental illness other than obvious retardation is fake.' 'Mental health professionals are godless quacks and simply a reason to excuse sin.'

My mother taught me that all mental health professionals operated without faith in God and therefore their advice was to be avoided like witchcraft. She held the key to truth and salvation, right?

The mere fact that I was admitting that I was afflicted with depression and needed help from a licensed psychologist would be a serious problem in any family discussion. So I was faced with a choice.

Continue living in denial and constant failure or abandon the notion of being accepted in my family, and look after my own health and well-being.

This required that I take a stand. This meant deciding that many ideas I had been 'raised with' were nonsense and came from my mom's lack of knowledge and experience.

The final but thorny road upward had begun.

# Chapter 82

# FINDING THE TRUTH

———————————————

I t might seem frighteningly obvious to the reader that I needed to change my belief system, but the prospect of abandoning my lifelong quest for approval from my mom was terrifying.

Terrifying because, above all things, my parents had instilled in me the incontrovertible fact that whatever they said was 'right.' And not just 'right,' but right with the conviction of God and salvation.

Most teenagers reject that sort of thinking outright. As they grow older they learn that their parents were smarter than they thought growing up.

Somehow I had been fooled into connecting my parents' truth with religious truth that I did accept. This made it impossible for me to separate them in any meaningful way until now.

As I write this I am 59 years old.

I have finally determined that the truth about God and his plan for us has nothing to do with my parent's life, lifestyle or opinions. They needed to work out their own religious observances and relationship with God and so do I.

Knowing that something absolutely had to change, I began tentatively to see a psychologist to explore my feelings. I had to understand how to put behind me the garbage I had been saddled with all my life.

Starting with those first visits, a little hope began to appear in my heart. I accepted his diagnosis of depression with trepidation, since that meant I was somehow "broken in my head."

I did a lot of research about depression and found out that the number of enormously creative people that had depression far outweighed the number who didn't. I began at least to note that I was in good company.

For the first time I began to consider the seriousness of my situation.

Many times in my life I had considered suicide, or had behaved in such a way that I was tempting fate and acting out a death wish. I was grateful I had failed.

I devoured various medical sites and scholarly journals where I read over and over again about causes and symptoms. I repeatedly had to answer yes to eight or nine of the typical questions posed to see if I was a depression candidate.

I finally accepted the fact that I had this condition, and that it had been with me for the last 35 years. Sometimes in the foreground and sometimes in remission.

After realizing that this was true, the next question for me was to figure out what this meant. What did I need to change and what could I do about this?

I incorrectly assumed that now that I knew, somehow everything would immediately change. I assumed that being aware of this condition was the gateway to freedom.

Knowledge is indeed, a first step in getting healthy. Not knowing about it, denying the possibility or not treating the depression that you have is a sure recipe for disaster. But knowing about it is only the first crucial step.

With this growing knowledge, I was able to see the cyclical repeating pattern of enormous success, feeling 'not good enough,' and unworthy, self-sabotage, and then creating insane crashes repeated over and over in my life.

I began to ask questions: 'Where did this come from?' 'Has this is always been true?' 'Was I born this way?' 'Can I fix it?'

With the right help, I began to understand what had likely created this situation.

I understood better how painful these cycles had been for me and those around me.

What made it worse, was the realization that at no time, during any of these big cycles of wild success and then 'crash and burn,' did I realize what the cause was.

Before I began to understand, I assumed (with the encouragement of everyone close to me,) that every time things went off the rails, it was simply a case of this horrible awful rotten person (me) doing stupid things because I didn't care about anyone.

Of course this kind of thinking simply added gasoline to an already raging fire of self-loathing in the ruined emotional landscape that was my life.

Knowing was the first step, but not the last. The path to healing is complicated and long. It has ups and downs and unexplained detours.

At least in my case, depression was to have one more romp with me in the woods before I finally got the pieces put together.

# Chapter 83

# NEAR DEATH—AGAIN

E very thriller movie has a moment near the end where the bad guy or the monster, who we thought was destroyed, suddenly jumps up one more time and nearly wipes out the good guy.

I don't know if this is a case of life imitating art or not. Be that as it may, it happened to me. Just like that. Depression roared back and tried one more time to claim my life.

Knowing the cause was good. Making sense of the cycles was critical. What was missing from my understanding of depression were the triggers.

I had no idea what triggered episodes of depression in me. I had begun to see some of the lead up phases of the cycles but didn't yet understand what the actual tipping points were.

It took and another major disaster before I understood what causes these events, at least for me. Fortunately this disaster lasted only two days. But once again, it brought me to death's door.

The occasion was a family gathering. My son's wedding. A joyful and celebratory occasion for the happy couple. Many members of both the bride and groom families would be present.

The day before the wedding was a rehearsal. Many of the participants gathered to walk through the ceremonies. I had been asked to emcee the reception after the wedding. I came to the rehearsal to get instructions and get organized.

Everything seemed to go well and the rehearsal was essentially perfect. The bride's family had prepared things flawlessly and thought of every detail. It was impressive.

My son's birth mother was also in attendance. This was the woman who had accused me of molesting children during the divorce. The same woman who lost custody of all her children.

After she lost custody she called my attorney and ask if my third wife would adopt the six younger children. The adoption took place. She was not even his mother anymore.

I never knew why she had given up her children for adoption. Some of the children had asked her in recent years. What I heard from the kids was that she blamed me for the adoption, saying that I was coming after her for child support and she couldn't pay it.

If a man gave up parental rights to his children because he didn't want to pay child support he would be considered a scumbag. But that's what she had done.

As an executive, I was highly compensated. At the time of the divorce the thought of asking for child support never crossed my mind. Somehow she had become fixated with the idea that I would. I have become the scapegoat.

Here is where the lingering effects of 'not good enough' and 'fundamentally flawed' came back to destroy me. In my mind, her giving the kids up for adoption was my fault.

If I hadn't been such a dirt bag and left the relationship, it never would've happened. The truth was that I had nothing to do with the adoption. She had initiated it by calling my attorney.

In addition, in private conversation with me, my son expressed a great deal of discomfort with her behavior. She was being pushy and demanding that she be treated as 'the mom,' even though she wasn't and he made it clear that he was very uncomfortable with her actions.

I felt guilty for that too.

All of that together took me down again. The confluence of the some of my kids being there brought reemerging guilt about everything being my fault. I was overwhelmed once again with the certainty that nothing would ever be okay again, and it was all my fault.

To the healthy person, blaming yourself for others actions might seem far-fetched or even ridiculous, but blaming yourself for everything and feeling worthless and hopeless is a very common piece of depression.

If you suffer from depression, you know exactly what I mean.

We left the rehearsal and went back to the hotel. Not much conversation took place between Joy and I. She sensed something was wrong and asked me what was going on.

I had not yet learned to share the growing feelings of terror. I couldn't talk about it. Part of the problem was that I felt guilty for feeling bad.

That's a bad reason if there ever was one. But anyone that thinks all this this emotional stuff makes perfect sense hasn't been there. I wasn't able to articulate my feelings and I kept them bottled up inside.

Joy had made an appointment to see a friend who lived nearby the day after the rehearsal. It was a girlfriend she hadn't seen in a couple of years. She had asked me to go with her, but, I declined saying that I had work to do. Against her better judgment, she went alone.

I sat in the hotel room stewing and fretting. My guilt and depression kicked in high gear. I did something I hadn't done for five years. I went out to get drunk. I walked to the liquor store. I don't remember what I purchased. I began drinking without stopping.

Joy came home and found the hotel room empty. I had left the computer open and the web browser showed the address of the nearest liquor store.

She came looking for me and found me but I wouldn't go with her back to the hotel. The story gets worse from here.

I spent the afternoon and evening wandering around drinking myself into oblivion.

Joy went out repeatedly looking for me, scared and heartbroken. Finally around midnight, without success, she came back to the hotel.

She found four strangers in our hotel room. I was passed out on the floor. The four strangers had found me face down in the gutter not far from our hotel.

As Providence would have it, these four people were two 'Good Samaritan' couples who gave their time to look for and help people in this area of the city.

Based on where they found me they figured out which hotel was mine. They came in and talked to the desk clerk. He recognized them because this was not the first time they had rescued someone in this area.

Somehow, apparently, I was able to stammer out my name. The desk clerk looked up the name and found that I was registered at hotel.

They took me up to my room and waited there until Joy arrived.

I don't remember any of this.

Chapter 84

# LUCKY TO BE ALIVE

They told her I was lucky to be alive. The area around the hotel was not particularly safe late at night. They chose this area to patrol to help with people just like me.

They told Joy that I could just as easily have been accosted by thugs and robbed and killed. They again reiterated to Joy how lucky I was that they found me since my fate otherwise would likely have been death.

I didn't find out about any of this until the next day. Once again, my life had been preserved.

The next day, Joy was frightened, hurt and angry. But she was grateful that I was alive. I had no explanation for what had happened. I could not understand my own behavior.

That's not to say that there are no consequences. We had planned to spend a romantic evening out in downtown Vancouver after the wedding rehearsal. My depressive episode cost us that memorable experience and created an emotional lead weight.

In addition, the next morning I was in no shape to go to church with my wife. We missed that experience together as well as any opportunity to go out to breakfast with each other or other family members before the wedding.

In the pictures at the wedding I certainly didn't look my best. My face was puffy and my eyes were red. One more mess.

But as far as the wedding was concerned, all of this drama went on behind the scenes. We attended the wedding, I was the emcee and it all went off without a hitch.

It was a lovely ceremony.

The bride and groom were very happy, the bride's family put on a great reception that everyone enjoyed in the afternoon and evening passed pleasantly for all the revelers.

It was beautiful and the newlyweds took off happily on their honeymoon.

I, however had something far more important to attend to. I absolutely had to understand what was driving this wild cycle of behavior and these unexplained cycles of self-loathing and self-abuse.

Finally, finally I was in a position to understand that no matter what it took, no matter what it cost, no matter what traditions or beliefs I needed to change, I must solve this problem.

If I was going to have a sane, successful life and create the future that I wanted, every effort had to go into this starting immediately.

All resistance was gone.

I now began open-mindedly studying this in earnest with a great effort first to understand and then to change whatever was necessary.

I immediately went to see a doctor where I described what happened and then I enlisted the help of a psychiatrist.

Chapter 85

# IS MEDICATION THE ANSWER?

answered a lot of questions. I described a lot of feelings. I described the lack
of feeling. I described the nature of the cycles of success and failure.

After a good bit of discussion the doctor prescribed an initial dose of a
particular antidepressant. She told me to try a couple of different doses over the
course of the prescription to see what had the most impact.

It's clear from what the doctor said and from what I have been able to learn
online that we don't have a deep understanding of what causes depression or
exactly what a depressed brain looks like.

There are all kinds of indicators and theories about neurotransmitters and
hippocampal damage and traumatic events and a number of other things that
seem to be common among those suffering from depression.

I also learned that there is deep disagreement among even highly respected
medical professionals about how depression should even be diagnosed
or treated.

At the end of the day there are simply different avenues to try. Different
chemicals, different combinations and different doses. Besides medication there
are also therapeutic, physical and emotional treatments and processes that are
sometimes effective

The massive disappointment for me is that none of these are aimed at 'curing'
depression. They only manage the symptoms.

I was also informed that antidepressants are always a bit tricky. Each person's reaction is different and some work well for a given individual and some work poorly.

None of this made me feel very confident. But underlying all of this was the absolute bedrock truth that the current situation was untenable. So doing nothing was not an option.

The doctor told me that it generally takes 4 to 6 weeks before there is a significant and stable change from the medication. So I expected to feel nothing for several weeks.

Eight years earlier I had briefly tried a different antidepressant during the time of my significant substance abuse.

I hadn't really given the medication a fair trial because I quit taking it so quickly.

I don't know why, but within a few hours of taking the first pill, I noticed something happening to me. This was a surprise since I expected to feel nothing for at least four weeks.

I have practiced meditation for 40 years and am extremely tuned into my body Perhaps that had something to do with it but I'm not sure.

By the afternoon of first day I began to notice that the way I was experiencing external stimulus was quite different.

Let me explain. By external stimulus I mean anything I saw or heard. After taking the medication, everything that 'touched' me felt softer. I'm not talking about my skin or fingers. I'm talking about touching me in terms of things I saw or heard.

Before taking the medication I felt like I lived in a world of sandpaper. Every single piece of information that touched me, particularly emotional content, felt abrasive. It felt like sandpaper rubbing against a road rash.

Any negative or imperfect circumstance in anyone's life was somehow my fault. I should already have anticipated this problem and fixed it before it occurred. Since that is impossible I nearly always felt like I had somehow failed.

I realize that such a statement doesn't make any sense and it might not be well explained, but that's the best I can do in a sentence or two. Those that have similar feelings will know exactly what I mean.

What I noticed about six hours after taking the medication is that the sandpaper was gone.

Things that normally would have triggered negative self-talk or even self-abuse were registered in a different fashion: simply as information that I did not feel responsible for.

It was as if a black cloud had been lifted from my mind. At the doctor's instruction I experimented a little bit with timing and dosage during the days that followed and landed on a schedule that seemed to work best for me.

Some people think that medication is the answer. For me it was just one piece. The other adjustments in my life, and figuring out the rest of the story were to come next.

The encouraging part was that with the cloud gone I could now think about things in a way that didn't trigger me. My perspective and ability to analyze things changed.

# Chapter 86

# TRUTH AND LOVE

L et me state right out of the gate that I do not believe that I would have been able to make this journey without my wife Joy. Her patience and love exceed all expectations.

Her ability to mirror my feelings and behavior so that I can understand them well is without equal. That's not to say this hasn't been difficult for her.

She has struggled because she worried that I will destroy myself. She has struggled because she has been called on to do things that are very difficult.

She has struggled wondering sometimes if all the effort is worth it. I can simply say that I am grateful beyond words that she chose to tough it out.

Since I had discarded all constraints about my approach to this problem, new insights came quickly. This opportunity created the arrival of what I call "The Third Epiphany."

I don't remember exactly when this realization came. I Think It developed gradually over a period of time, but at the same time it feels like it came all at once.

A lightning bolt like the first two revelations. I suddenly remember feeling enlightened at one point and being able to state it this way:

"I CAN BE ME."

Without apology, without constraint. I have innate gifts and talents. I have worth and power and at my very best I am 'me' to the core. That is when

I can do the most good, be the best person and give and receive love in the most powerful way.

Obviously, there are societal and moral constraints to the extremes of this statement, but I am not talking about those extremes.

I AM talking about discarding all the old baggage, paradigms and nonsense I had accepted from my formative years.

I AM talking about exploring, developing and maximizing the gifts and talents I have in a positive and productive way that serves those around me, makes a good living, creates fun and joy and leads to a happy and productive life.

This might be fairly obvious to those not living in depression, but for me, it was a massive revelation.

When I combined this monumental learning with the first two: "I Am In Control," and "I Am Enough," these three statements have allowed me to claim control over my life and emotions.

Gone are the old judgments and stories. Gone are the false guilt and especially meaningless shame. Gone are the imagined and real noises of disapproval.

I suppose they are still there, but my frequency tuning can no longer hear them. I no longer care what they broadcast anyway.

The medication has been very helpful, but I do not believe it would be effective without the final realization added to the first two epiphanies. Together these have formed a framework for a healthy new life.

At least it is so for me.

One thing I have learned about this affliction is that every circumstance is unique. I do not pretend to have an answer for all people. I do not pretend to have the silver bullet.

What I know for sure is what worked for me and what gave me the power to grab my life and turn it into a beautiful symphony instead of a strident clash of discord and pain.

That's not to say there aren't struggles. That's not to say there are days that I feel awful and want to give up. That's not to say that things don't still trigger depressive episodes.

What it does say is that I have a new set of tools. I have a new outlook. I have a new measuring tape that lets me frame the events around me in a way that makes sense now.

# Chapter 87

# RE-CREATION

R e-creating my life had to start almost the beginning. Not like learning to walk again. But I had to start with some pretty fundamental basics.

I discovered very quickly that I had never realized what it meant to have a friend. A true friend. Many of you reading this may have had that great blessing.

If you have a true friend, I applaud you. True friendship goes two ways and cannot be maintained in a one-sided manner.

I finally figured out how to have my first and best friend. It's a funny thing being in your 50s and finally having a "best friend." But that's the truth of my reality.

I finally have a friend I can talk to, a friend I don't have to be afraid of. Up till that point, every relationship I experienced had contingencies. Love was conditional.

I also realized that growing up I had never been allowed to experiment and form my own opinions. I was told what was right and wrong and there were simply no deviations.

Clothes I could wear, hairstyles I could adopt, music I could listen to, books I could read, opinions I could explore or talk about, and on and on and on.

I realize now that, except for a few personal tastes like food, my opinions about many things, about truth, fairness, right and wrong and other fundamental issues weren't even mine.

I grew up in a framework where everything was completely predetermined. You are only okay if you are following the rules and fit in the box. Somebody else's rules. Somebody else's box.

There was no room for question, there was no opportunity for discussion. As a kid, I didn't have options. I stuffed my feelings and followed the rules.

It was as if there was this unspoken mandate—'You can only be acceptable if you conform to this 'certain set of beliefs and behaviors' and then you are allowed the glory of my approval and love.'

While God may be able to determine right and wrong, it is outside the purview of any person on the earth to make such a declaration and cram it down the throat of another.

Because of fear I had given up my privilege to learn and grow. I had consequently denied myself the opportunity to create a meaningful framework for my own life.

A big piece of my healing and re-creation came from my ceremonial 'Declaration of Independence' from these old scripts and rules that had been beat into me as a child.

I actually wrote out a long list of my own declarations. I wrote out a declaration of independence from people and ideas that had kept me locked up and bound.

I read it out loud with full emotion and power and then in a ceremony burned the list of ropes, chains and locks to symbolically demonstrate the freedom I now demanded, needed and cherished.

There have been many such ceremonies and many such declarations. Each time I find myself in a situation that feels like the old paradigms and behaviors take control, I now have the tools to ask myself important questions.

Why am I actually feeling this way? Where do the beliefs and ideas come from that are driving these feelings? Are they absolutely true? Are there adjustments I need to make that will serve me better?

These and many similar questions have become important tools in creating freedom and in restoring my creative power. Now I can do the things I came to do, sing the songs I came to sing, love the way I was meant to love and enjoy this beautiful world and the people in it to the fullest.

The change has taken a lot of getting used to. I had lived my life in complete emotional isolation and never opened my heart to anyone, for fear of rejection.

It has been a hard thing to begin to be completely bare and transparent. But hard or not, I'm excited at the opportunity and certainly up for the adventure.

I also had to learn that it was possible to have dedication and loyalty in a relationship.

In every relationship, partners learn things about each other that can be twisted and manipulated. If there is any sharing between partners whatsoever, information is shared that can be damaging.

When my relationships failed, every partner except my first wife strained to remember and exaggerate every possible flaw and evil in my character or behavior.

It may be a normal thing in divorce, but two of my three divorces were over-the-top with exaggerated negativity and vile accusation. Truth was the first casualty. Nothing was held truly confidential or inviolate.

It may seem strange to some but I did not reciprocate. Even though I had videotapes and documents that would have destroyed careers and reputations, I never used them. I'm glad I didn't.

I'm not sure why I didn't fight fire with fire.

My true learning about relationships from my second and third marriages was simply that that openness is dangerous and loyalty is imaginary.

If I hadn't had the blessing of finding Joy I think I would have concluded that there was no such thing as true friendship and loyalty.

# Chapter 88

# A NEWNESS OF LIFE

~~~~~~~~~~~~~~~~~~~~~~~~~~~~~~~~~

For the first time in my life, I have the freedom to explore myself, to acknowledge those parts that are broken and get help, and go about the process of healing.

I am now blessed with the opportunity to do this in an atmosphere of love and patience even when things get scary.

The value of that gift is priceless. The effect of that supportive framework cannot be measured. For those who live with depressed persons, your ability to remain calm, loving and patient is paramount.

I'm not giving advice or passing any judgments about your situations. I realize that sometimes it may not be possible, but for me it was life-changing.

I'm not pretending that Joy just ignored problems or quietly pretended everything was okay. Quite the contrary. Living with the depressive can be miserable and painful.

But she was willing to stay in the conversation and in the battles while we figured out how to make things work. She focused on the long view.

For the first time in my life, I have permission to be myself. It is such a huge framework change that it took me a while to figure out who I was. Such freedom had never been allowed before. I had always had to play a particular role instead of acting from who I was.

This freedom has created some other significant changes. I was able to break open that area of my life that had been 'paved over' so many years before. I mentioned in an earlier chapter the decision that I made in my 20s to 'pave over' my creative side and not pursue music because it was 'evil.'

With Joy's help and the help of the psychologist I was seeing, I was able to rip up that pavement and explore fully the creative gifts that I have. As a result, I have put out several albums of new music in the last few years.

More importantly, I was able to figure out how to my combine my interests with the discoveries along this journey. I wrote this book so I could use these painful learnings in a positive way to bless the lives of those who have been afflicted with depression and those who help us.

The next thing I learned was the meaning of loyalty.

I learned the true loyalty is not conditional. I learned the true loyalty allows you to depend on another person regardless of circumstance. That was a foreign concept to me.

My entire life had been one of being unable to truly depend on others. When things are good, no problem, but when it's really on the line nobody's home.

As I near the end of the story it feels important to think about and describe the core essential elements that made all the difference for me.

You will have to adapt these elements to create their own path to a stable life. Maybe you will have a completely different list.

I share them here in the hopes that there will be something here that will make your journey easier whether you suffer from depression or love someone who does.

I know for sure that there are four things without which I would not have succeeded thus far in my battle with the monster of depression.

First, Divine Help:

- I have come to know without question there is a God.
- In his own way in time he is willing and does provide blessings and opportunity in our lives.
- He certainly saved my life on more than one occasion.
- He brought me the one true companionship that I needed to create a beautiful life.

- I have come to know and depend fully upon the saving grace of Jesus Christ.

I'm not trying to prescribe a particular religious observance or tell you what to believe. But I would not be complete without fully and freely acknowledging the significant role that God has played in my recovery.

I don't pretend to understand all the details of how God interacts with man on the earth. I just know that when I desperately looked for help, it came. Not usually like I expected or wanted, but it came.

Second, A Willing Heart.

I have been stubborn and self-righteous sometimes. I have been totally discouraged and desperate to die at other times. Depression and the certainty that I was 'not good enough' shaped my life in more ways than I will ever even realize.

But the times that my heart was open and willing was when those instances of divine help came. If I had ignored them or refused the message, the outcome would obviously have been different.

I struggled terribly sometimes with how to implement what I thought I was learning. How I have interpreted my epiphanies has certainly changed through the decades.

But I was always keenly aware that the help that had come from above. I was willing to make changes in order to respond to the call.

I have also become willing to seek and apply professional help and treatment from both doctors and shrinks. Learning a willingness to throw off old stories and be open to medication and therapy has been critical.

Third, Finding or Creating Support

For much of my life I lived essentially in isolation. I went to large public schools. I went to a gigantic university. I was married and had children. I went and visited family when I was on the good list. But I was still alone.

Really needing to lean on someone else was both scary and somehow not okay. As a kid my parents were the source of fear, and my siblings couldn't be trusted because they would tattle whenever it suited their needs.

Either because I was younger then kids in my class or because I was physically and emotionally abused or because I was awkward or because I was afraid, I never learned to create real friendships among people at school or at church or in the neighborhood.

We weren't really encouraged to have friends that were not part of the church because they were going to lead us to do evil, so that really limited the choices.

For me, finding a friend changed my life in lasting and profound ways. Having someone to teach me basic skills like having a friend and the meaning of loyalty was critical.

The blessing of a friend who stands by me while I experiment with remedies about how to fix my life has changed the game.

Most importantly, Joy has created the stability and framework to build this. I lacked unconditional love all my life and she was the cure.

Fourth, Absolute Determination

Depression sucks. It comes and goes. It strikes without warning and sometimes for reasons that only become obvious after the fact.

Determination to get to a different and state is a non-negotiable piece of the puzzle.

Commitment is one of those funny things. We talk about commitment. We pretend we have it, but most people give up when the going gets tough.

I know I gave up several times and got lost sometimes in the shuffle. But underneath it all, somehow, somewhere I knew there was a better way than the path I was on.

I knew that somewhere there was an answer. When that opportunity came I grabbed it and would not let go. Carpe diem.

# Chapter 89

# A COMMON STORY

The word 'common' has at least two meanings. Common can mean something that is 'frequent' and it can also mean something that is 'shared.'

Since I started to tell the story of my depression and be open about its causes and consequences many wonderful things have begun to happen.

So many people that I talk to have similar stories to relate. We have a shared experience. They tell me stories about themselves or about some other loved one in their life.

A father, a mother, a sister, a brother, a friend, a spouse or significant other, someone that is near and dear to them that has been affected by depression.

The content of the story is strikingly similar. The pain, the confusion, the addictions, the thoughts of suicide, the struggle for meaning.

This is our 'common story.' A story that we share both in the nature of the events and in the nature of the feelings that are part of the process.

This is one of the most important things I wanted to accomplish by writing this book. Sharing stories, raising awareness and creating action. Moving us all past the misunderstanding and the stigma and the hiding and the blaming.

A typical reaction I hear is just like the one from my mother. 'You're blaming me for your sins.' Another version of this is 'you're just excusing your awful behavior.'

The truth is that I would not have walked the same path without depression as my companion. I would not have made the same choices, I would have had a different viewpoint and different opinions, leading to completely different actions and outcomes.

What this different person would have looked like is a fantasy I can't afford to indulge in. When I do, it simply creates guilt, shame and blame.

If you suffer from depression I know you have experienced some of these feelings. You have experienced some of these accusations, you have experienced the same guilt, shame and blame that I just described.

We have a common bond.

With that common bond, we also have both the opportunity and the responsibility to make a difference. I wrote this book to begin that journey for me.

In addition to this book, there are two albums of music I have composed and recorded talking about the two sides of the depression coin.

One of these albums is called 'Songs of Promise and Power.' The other is called 'Songs From the Dark Place'. Together they constitute my musical view of the same journey.

Whatever your method of expression could be or might be, use it and choose to help me participate in the solution.

The other meaning of 'common' is something that is 'frequent.'

I haven't read all the studies. What I have read suggests that fully 20% of the population in at least the United States and Canada suffers from depression at some point in their lives. In that same population, nearly 20 million people have depression right this minute.

It's a pretty common condition. It's a serious condition. In my own life and experience it has caused enormous heartache and pain and suffering for me and all those that got hit with the shrapnel.

I think it's time to do something more and so I wrote this book and recorded this music to make a dent in the problem and lend my support to the solution.

# Chapter 90

# FORGIVENESS

A painful but interesting thing that has happened since I began talking about my depression is the rejection syndrome.

Particularly those close to me seem to fall in this group. They can't accept the truth that I tell and so they either reject me by remaining silent, reject me by telling me how to fix it or reject me by telling me it's not true.

One of the most uninformed responses about the condition involves the word 'forgiveness.' Particularly from my brothers and sisters I keep getting the question 'Why haven't you forgiven our mom yet?'

An uninformed question at best. They seem to think that forgiveness will be the only key to healing my life. What it really feels like they're saying is they want me to hurry up and forgive so we can stop talking about this problem.

Forgiveness is a critical piece of the healing, but only one small piece. They are completely missing miss the two separate aspects of the problem.

One part is indeed forgiveness of the perpetrator. Sometimes that is possible for a victim to forgive the perpetrator and sometimes not. Every case is different.

In my case, I have long since forgiven my mom for the abuse she inflicted on me growing up. I have no idea what caused her to behave in such a terrible fashion.

I can make up some reasons and pretend some context into existence, but since I don't really know, it wouldn't mean much. So I don't think that's a useful pursuit.

I hold no anger and no grudge. I am not sitting on pins and needles waiting for her to apologize. In all truth, that will likely never happen.

The one time in my life I broached the subject with her, she reacted angrily and said 'You are trying to blame your sins on me.' No dear mother, I'm blaming your sins on you.

The second part of the issue is the molding and shaping that takes place when traumatic events occur.

If a person is bitten by a dog several times, they probably develop a fear of dogs. They may forgive the owner, forgive the dog and hold no grudges.

But the shaping of their feelings, manifest by being afraid of dogs, or even having a physical reaction when they hear a dog barking, is still a reality.

Overcoming that problem is an entirely separate process than forgiving the owners or forgiving the dog or no longer being angry or hateful or bitter toward anyone involved. It is separate, it takes different work and a different approach.

Forgiveness is not the key to this part of the problem.

When I speak to my brothers and sisters, it's like they are blaming the victim.

If someone runs a red light and smashes my car and I get injured, several things have to happen. I can forgive the driver, I can choose not to prosecute or sue, but after those decisions are made I still have to fix my car and go to the hospital to heal my broken bones.

Harping on me about whether or not I have forgiven the driver has nothing to do with healing my broken bones, learning to walk again, and overcoming fear that I might have as I approach intersections.

I might develop a traumatic fear of driving or any number of other problems might show up because of such an accident.

It is as if they think that the forgiveness of the perpetrator somehow heals all of the long-term rehabilitation I have to do because of the wreck.

If I lose a leg in such an accident, the leg is gone, no matter what. Forgiving the perpetrator means I no longer hold bitterness, anger and resentment toward that person, but it doesn't change the fact that I am without a leg for the rest of my life.

The kind of attitude they have demonstrated simply underscores the stigma, the lack of understanding and the lack of an intelligent approach to dealing with the issues around mental illness.

Clearly both in my family and as a society we have an enormous amount of work to do.

Chapter 91

# WHAT NOW?

This sky is blue and it is cold outside this morning. That's unusual for southern Arizona, but it happens sometimes. It actually froze the last few nights.

The book is written. Many of the songs are written and most are recorded. Soon the book will be published and the albums available and then getting the story told about what has happened so far will be finished.

But telling the story of what happened so far is only the beginning of this process. I know my experience and journey with depression is not over. This goes on forever.

Like I said in the beginning: I'm not an expert at the diagnosis or treatment of depression, but I have become an expert in living with it and figuring out how to manage its ongoing interference.

With the benefit of the four things I listed in an earlier chapter, I have come to a place in my life where I can live despite this condition, at least so far.

I am hopeful that my ability to manage it will be an ongoing truth. And I expect not only to live my own life fully but also to create a huge reservoir of help and support for others.

Having finally learned what it feels like to fully experience feelings and let them run their course is a revelation. It's a funny thing to say, but feelings just are. They come from all kinds of sources.

The only feelings I had known were fear, shame, guilt, loneliness and isolation. Consequently, I eliminated feelings from my life. It's a wonderful experience to perceive and enjoy the range of emotions that accompany the human condition.

I have also learned to share those emotions in a real and deep way. This has had profound implications on my ability to form connections with others.

First is my wife, Joy. She was the lead character in the drama of my healing. My ability to experience and express feelings with her has grown exponentially. I can now understand expression of feelings from her and others in a healthy way.

Finally, coming to a place where I can understand what has happened to me the last 30 years has been profound and cathartic. Understanding the driver for the behaviors, experiences and lack of feelings has been almost magic.

This arrival has kindled a huge desire in me to help others with depression.

Recently a prominent actor committed suicide. This suicide was blamed on the depression he suffered for decades.

My study has revealed that there are many prominent figures who struggle with depression. Some successfully and some unsuccessfully. It seems to particularly affect the creative mind.

Those who are the most creative are often the most self-critical and suffer the deepest from the fear, lack of confidence, need to hide and the many other emotional descriptions that accompany the emptiness we call depression.

This book and the two albums are just the beginning of my effort to de-stigmatize this condition, create more open dialogue and do everything I can to raise the discussion and the consciousness of this widespread affliction.

I want something different to happen. I'm going to do everything that I can to make it so.

I wrote this book to tell a story. I did that because that's how it unfolded. For the longest time I was completely unaware that I was afflicted with depression. I simply thought that the lack of feeling in my life was normal.

I naively thought that the extreme highs and incredible bottomless pits of my experience were simply part of the normal process of life. I bought the line that I was a failure.

Gratefully, I have learned that those extremes and particularly the depth and duration of the crashes is one of the fundamental hallmarks of depression.

Even though our knowledge is not complete, I am grateful for what we do know. I am grateful for treatments both in the form of medication, and in the form of therapy.

But most of all my gratitude is for my learning from what happened in my life.

Getting to that level of awareness gave me the greatest tool of all. It has given me a perspective and an understanding of the crazy path of my life. It also strengthened my determination to live in a healthy way myself and help others do the same.

The story will continue to unfold as the years and decades stretch out into the future. I will keep telling the story. You can follow it at www.tightropeofdepression.com.

I find myself now overwhelmed with gratitude for the perspective and freedom that have come to me throughout this difficult journey.

I do not know how well the tools, practices and processes that I have used will help to others with the same condition, but I share them in hopes that they will be useful.

However, what I do know is that clients that I coach in my business have achieved significant benefits from the perspectives and learning that have come as a result of this decade's long journey.

The purpose of this book has been to awaken you and cause you to think deeply. Perhaps to scare you. Perhaps to make you ask some hard questions and demand answers.

By taking you on the journey that I traveled. I hope to give you insights into your world by learning what happened to me. I didn't know what was going on in my life. Maybe you don't understand some of your life either. If this book helps you at all, I am happy.

My deepest hope is that you will find real and lasting benefit in these pages.

That you will find some tools and insight that will help you, some encouragement to know that there is healing and relief if you are willing to do the work, make the changes and pay the price.

I invite you to contact me in any one of the ways listed below if I might be of service to you. Wherever you are in your journey, either as one afflicted or as a loved one of someone affected by the monster we call depression.

In the epilogue I will give details of exactly what practices I did and still do today as a regular routine to help keep me productive, happy and joyful.

If you wish to have more resources to help you or want to contact me, here are the best ways:

www.tightropeofdepression.com

www.breakthecagenow.com

www.kellanfluckiger.com

email: coachkellanfluckiger@gmail.com or info@kellanfluckiger.com

# EPILOGUE—HELPING OTHERS

The frontiers of what is 'fixable' keep moving. This is true for both ailments of the body and of the mind.

Experimental processes, drugs and other treatment methods continue to allow us to extend our capability to repair that which is functioning improperly or broken.

The purpose of this epilogue is to give you everything that I have learned so far about the effects of depression and the tools that I use to create a whole and centered life.

I am not giving medical advice, I am not a doctor. I am not a psychologist and so I am not giving 'counseling advice.' I am telling you everything I learned and explaining exactly what I do to manage this disease that debilitated my life for three decades.

Let's start with some facts that we know. I'm not claiming these are the only contributors. But they are some really obvious problems that played a big role for me.

1. Stress is a killer. We all have some, sometimes a lot. The negative effects of stress are more associated with the length of time and frequency and less with the severity of one incident.

2. Anger is a killer. It is also a normal emotion. Like stress, the intensity is not the issue but more the duration and frequency of the feeling.

3. Experiencing emotions is essential. Stuffing emotions, pretending them away or failing to deal with them is a lethal contributor to depression.

4. Patterns and experiences from childhood have a long-lasting effect on our behavior. Pretending them away or acting like they don't matter is both foolish and counterproductive.

5. Living as a "victim," or allowing yourself to live in the "victim role," for long periods of time plays havoc with your view of reality.

6. Refusing to acknowledge a problem, pretending that what you're doing is okay or failing to admit the need for some help is simply asking for it to get worse or go on forever.

My own experience with all of these things was substantial. Every single one of those behaviors played an enormous role in my life, especially during my formative years and the years of active addiction.

I was constantly under stress from not being good enough. I found myself often angry with no way to express it. Expressing emotion, in any way not "approved," was frowned on and punished. The book is a journey of my experience with these six things.

There is some research that suggests that genetics play a role in a predisposition to depression.

The bottom line is that some combination of environmental factors and experiences in my life created my decades of experience with depression.

In doing research for writing this book I have become extremely excited about some fairly recent medical findings. Perhaps you have heard about neuroplasticity. This is the word that describes the ability of the brain to create new neural pathways.

Additional recent research seems to indicate that parts of the brain can be repaired. This is contrary to older thinking and medical opinion which suggested that the brain, once damaged was irreparable.

The combination of the six factors described earlier, and perhaps others, damage the brain's ability to regulate neurotransmitters. The big ones are serotonin, norepinephrine, and dopamine.

What I also learned from reading many medical journals, and from having lengthy discussions with doctors and psychiatrists, is that high cortisol levels associated with many of the factors listed above damage parts of the brain. This damage has consequences.

On a cognitive level this damage makes it hard to disengage from a negative mindset. Knowing this now explains a lot about my experiences.

I was regularly caught up for hours and even days in an endless loop of negative thinking about how badly I had acted in a given situation and subsequently assumed that everything that happened was all my fault.

This loop was often exacerbated by family members and those in my intimate circle who would jump right on the bandwagon and blame everything on me.

I was not wise enough to understand this was a sign of their own insecurity and brokenness and not a statement of fact. Because I could not disengage from a negative mindset I simply accepted these things as reality.

Another finding I read about was that such brain damage from excessive cortisol also leads to a bias toward negativity and away from positive experiences and emotions. It even creates a bias against a positive interpretation of neutral experiences.

It is not difficult for me than to look at these findings and understand how I ended up in the various situations in my life. It is no longer hard for me to understand the coping behaviors and addictions that came and went to mask the pain of constant negativity and self-loathing.

The exciting news is that the brain seems to be able to repair itself if we do the right things. There seems to be certain activities and certain behaviors we can control that produce BDNF (brain derived neurotrophic factor.)

This substance is a brain protein that is highly active in the growth and differentiation of new neurons and synapses. Simply put, it helps your grow and repair your brain.

Over time this 'BDNF' allows the brain to repair and heal. This could mean that permanent dependence on mood altering drugs or SSRIs may not be necessary.

Again, I'm not giving medical advice just reporting on what I have found in my own struggle against the monster. For me this is all great news.

So here is the list of the things I did to get my life organized and create a peaceful and powerful life. The purpose of the list is to give an insight of what worked for me. Hopefully this will benefit you too.

This list is not in order of importance, because the order of importance for me would certainly not be the order of importance for you. The order of importance for you would be related to your own experience and how you got in a state of severe depression.

1. TALK. It was forever before I learned that I had to talk about this stuff. I was unwilling to express or explore any of the things that I was feeling. Wrong thinking was punished. Wrong speech was punished even more. Depression itself was wrong. Psychologists were evil and everything could be handled just by sucking it up.

2. BE OPEN. This is related to talking but it is easy to talk and not be truthful. It is easy to talk around topics and talk about them in generalities without explaining the depth of your own feeling.

3. BE HONEST. For me this was extremely difficult. I grew up learning to lie about everything because that was the only way I kept out of trouble.

   The problem was that the habit of lying carried over into my adult life and I found it easier to lie about everything because it 'kept me out of trouble.'

4. FIND SUPPORT. If you don't have someone you can talk to or be open or honest with then change friends, go somewhere else or change your circumstances. That may sound harsh. But the choice is between living in misery forever or making some changes so you can get healthy.

5. BE WILLING TO CHANGE. This might seem obvious. But often we are more comfortable with 'the devil we know than the devil we don't.'

6. BELIEVE A BETTER FUTURE IS POSSIBLE. This is a very difficult one and can only be accomplished with the help of others. When you live forever in depression, the idea of a future without it is impossible to conceive.

   This is particularly true when the depression is severe. Openly talking with others and understanding their experience will allow you to believe that something different is possible.

7. LEARN TO MEDITATE. Recent medical research demonstrates CONCLUSIVELY that those who learn to meditate and meditate regularly have improved brain function, reduced tendency to depression and are able to recover more completely and quickly.

   However, there are different kinds of meditation and learning to meditate in a fashion that is helpful for depression is ESSENTIAL.

   I practiced meditation for 40 years, but because I did not know I was depressed, I was not using this awesome tool effectively. The minute I learned what was going on and changed the way I did it the results were magic.

   If you are interested in my help, reach out.

8. GET HELP. For me this was finally going to see a psychiatrist and telling him about the number of times I had nearly died intentionally or unintentionally.

   It was finally being willing to talk to a psychiatrist and psychologist about the brutal upbringing I had. It was finally admitting I needed some help and being willing and open to accept the suggestions. This included being willing to try medication. It has been my experience that medication is NOT a complete solution, but only part of a comprehensive approach.

   Medication was only one tiny step in a long and complicated process. For me I had 30 years of a terrible pattern to unravel.

   Thirty years of believing I was at fault for everything. Thirty years of living in a loop of negativity and accepting blame and responsibility for every negative outcome. Thirty years of desperately struggling for the approval from someone I would never get it from.

For me, the medication quickly allowed me to see my situation from a different perspective. It did not dismantle the 30 years of bad habits or bad feelings.

It did allow me to begin to chip away at that wall of past habit with a new tool. It allowed me to understand that my perspective had been wrong. It allowed me to shed behaviors and thinking patterns that were horrible and damaging.

It allowed me to choose a new view. It allowed me to choose to look up.

I still needed and continue to need to choose that new view on purpose and then continue to dismantle the 30 year brick wall.

Fortunately it's faster taking it down that it was putting it up.

This is partly because I understand what's going on now. This is partly because of the medication. It is partly because I am doing all of the other things that I listed before and after this point that helped me reconstruct my reality.

I write this part in such length because we live in a society that is so married to the idea that a pill solves everything. The medication did something for me. It simply allowed me to stand in a new place and look at the situation differently.

All the work after that was still mine to do, but I was able to do it because I had a new understanding.

9. GET A COACH WHO UNDERSTANDS. This is one of the reasons I am expanding my coaching practice to focus part of it on depression.

I had an interview with a prospective client just yesterday. It was astounding how much secrecy was in his life. Of course, he had no one to talk to. Of course, he had no one to be honest with.

The stigma associated with this illness is staggering, embarrassing and debilitating. We don't want to talk about it and we treat people who have it like they are some kind of lepers.

Even leprosy has a cure. The fact that we can't have an open and meaningful dialogue about this is a travesty, a shameful indictment of our attitudes.

Sometimes I get asked what the differences between mental health professional and a coach. There is a huge difference between a psychologist, psychiatrist or therapist and a coach.

Both functions are necessary.

Mental health professionals diagnose and prescribe treatment for mental illness. For those affected by mental illness, this is usually the first critical step.

A therapist made function in a number of roles. I know therapists that also perform coaching and others who simply define therapy more narrowly. Some therapy does not provide objectives, but is simply a reflective environment for you to solve your own problems.

A coach does what a coach does best. He helps you set your goals. He holds you accountable to your commitments. He watches your performance and make sure you get over the goal line.

It's important not to confuse the objectives of these different functions.

If you are interested in my help, reach out.

10. CHANGE YOUR DIET AND OTHER HABITS. Of the 10 things listed here, this is the one where I probably still have the most work. There have been many studies showing that diet and the other habits discussed below are related to our overall health and may affect depression.

There is scientific and medical research that demonstrates that certain things are a disaster for your brain chemistry. If you are prone to depression, have depression or have ever had depression it could be dangerous to violate these rules listed below.

a. Quit eating sugar. It is in almost all processed foods and it is a disaster for your body in many ways.

b. Eliminate alcohol. Alcohol is more powerful than sugar and it destroys brain cells and neurotransmitters. This is probably particularly poignant for those with depression since alcohol is a frequent refuge from the pain.

c.  Eliminate dim lighting. Bright lighting has a positive effect on the brain and the mood.

d.  Experience more laughter. Laughter creates all kinds of good chemistry in the brain and helps in many ways to change the focus we depressives have on negativity.

e.  Eliminate Toxic people from your life. Easy to say and hard to do. Your life depends on it. This may require frank and hard conversations, but the alternative is unthinkable.

f.  Make radical changes to eliminate or mitigate stress. There are tools and processes that help ELIMINATE Stress, not just MANAGE it. If you want my help, reach out.

g.  Engage in long periods of exercise. Long walks, extended jogging, long bike rides are far better than short intense exercise with respect to depression.

The findings suggest that this type of exercise produces the chemistry necessary to make the "BDNF" of in your brain. This is the chemical that allows the actual healing of the brain.

For me, this news about brain repair is the most exciting part about my healing journey. The idea that there is something to make it actually "better," instead of just applying Band-Aids in the form of medication is a very hopeful and encouraging fact.

h.  Make sure your diet includes:
    1.  omega-3 fats
    2.  low glycemic foods
    3.  vitamin D and folic acid
    4.  selenium
    5.  antioxidants
    6.  This list will change quickly and perhaps radically depending on new discoveries. Pay attention to ongoing developments.

Any of your foodie friends will be able to help you figure out what to do to make sure this dietary piece is in order.

Depression is not a trivial matter. It dramatically affected three decades of my life. It kills millions. It is no respecter of persons, wealth or status.

Statistically it seems to be on the rise. One estimate I saw said that there are probably 19 million people in the US at any given time who suffer from this disease and that over the entire population, probably one in five suffer at some time in their lives.

Depression comes and goes, strikes without warning and crushes without remorse. Understanding yourself, your life and the things that you can do to control the triggers and the healing elements are critical steps to manage this condition.

Above all, don't be afraid to get help and to talk about it. It has gone undiscussed, undiagnosed and untreated far too long. It has killed far too many people. The shrapnel from those affected has hurt far too many lives for us to remain silent any longer.

Perhaps you suspect you have depression. Perhaps you know someone with it or maybe you just want more information. Don't just think about it. Take the steps necessary to find out and then do something.

My greatest desire is to help and bless others who are or have been affected this way. I am now in a position to give back and am dedicated to making a huge difference against this tragic killer.

There is nothing I love more than seeing people recover, get their lives back, grow, clear out the fog and see clearly again.

Nothing will happen until we take action.

Join me.

# A free eBook edition is available with the purchase of this book.

**To claim your free eBook edition:**

1. Download the Shelfie app.
2. Write your name in upper case in the box.
3. Use the Shelfie app to submit a photo.
4. Download your eBook to any device.

## Shelfie

A free eBook edition is available
with the purchase of this print book.

CLEARLY PRINT YOUR NAME ABOVE IN UPPER CASE

**Instructions to claim your free eBook edition:**
1. Download the Shelfie app for Android or iOS
2. Write your name in **UPPER CASE** above
3. Use the Shelfie app to submit a photo
4. Download your eBook to any device

## Print & Digital Together Forever.

Snap a photo          Free eBook          Read anywhere

## The Morgan James
## Speakers Group

We connect Morgan James published authors with live and online events and audiences whom will benefit from their expertise.